Suffering from Cheerfulness
The Best Bits from
THE WIPERS TIMES

To John Billham

in memory of past days

from the Writer

JC Roberts

Dedication reproduced courtesy of the Imperial War Museum

Suffering from Cheerfulness
The Best Bits from
THE WIPERS TIMES

Foreword
by IAN HISLOP
Introduction by
MALCOLM BROWN

This edition published in 2010 by Little Books Ltd,
Notting Hill, London W11 3QW

10 9 8 7 6 5 4 3 2 1

Introduction © 2007 by Malcolm Brown
Design and layout copyright © 2010 by Little Books Ltd

A CIP catalogue record for this book is available
from the British Library.

ISBN: 978 1 906251 291

The author and publisher will be grateful for any information that
will assist them in keeping future editions up-to-date. Although all
reasonable care has been taken in the preparation of this book,
neither the publisher, editors nor the author can accept any
liability for any consequences arising from the use thereof, or the
information contained therein.

Printed by Toppan Leefung (China) Limited

FOREWORD

'Oh, to be in Belgium now that winter's here.' This is the unmistakable voice of *The Wipers Times*, and ninety years since it first appeared I am delighted to see the complete collection back in print. This extraordinary magazine was written, printed, distributed and read by British soldiers serving in the trenches of the Western Front during the First World War. It was produced on an abandoned printing press salvaged from the ruins of Ypres – hence the title with the classic British mispronunciation – and was an immediate success from its first edition. It continued to appear throughout the war and was subsequently reissued in the following years of peace. Its extraordinary mix of jokes, sarcasm, black humour and sentimental poetry make it a unique record of the period. It is quite literally laughing in the face of death, with jokes about flame-throwers and gas attacks from the troops who were facing them. It is also very rude about senior officers, the home front and the organization of the war. It is *Blackadder* for real and an obvious forerunner of magazines like *Private Eye*.

I have long been an admirer of *The Wipers Times*, and once made a documentary about it for BBC Radio Four called Are We As Offensive As We Might Be? This was a question which staff officers from headquarters used to ask troops in the front line when they thought that they were insufficiently keen to go over the top and attack the Germans. It became a sort of catchphrase for the writers of the magazine, who would ask each other, '*Are we as offensive as we might be?*'

I thought that this was very British – as was the fact that the editor, a very talented man called Captain Fred Roberts, was working on the copy for an edition of the magazine called *The Somme Times* during the Battle of the Somme. He was correcting proofs in the trench and yet he went on to win the

Military Cross for bravery in that very battle. That's an editor who commands respect.

Roberts wrote that war was mostly about 'wallowing in a ditch', but he and his fellow writers managed to create something finer, funnier and more life-enhancing from their grim situation. I think that *The Wipers Times* has often been unjustly ignored and that it is actually firmly in the great tradition of British comic literature. The authors would probably have laughed at that idea, too.

Ian Hislop

INTRODUCTION

There's no denying that the First World War has had a bad press over recent decades.

It's seen as a catalogue of horrors, as four and a half years of appalling misery during which no soldier smiled or chuckled or dared to dream that he would ever get back to dear old Blighty. But warfare has always had its lighter side. As a former Tommy wrote in a memoir quoted in my first book on this war: 'Even in the most dire of circumstances, shell-fire, machine-gun fire, knee deep in mud and water, with short rations and pay-day just a distant memory, most of us still found time for a laugh and a joke.' Wilfred Owen himself, arguably the supreme laureate of Western Front disenchantment, was not above stating: 'Merry it was to laugh there/Where death becomes absurd and life absurder.'

The Wipers Times was a laugh and a joke on the grand scale. The war produced a mass of trench newspapers and journals: in effect, school magazines for a new dispensation in which playing fields had become killing fields and the blowing of a whistle meant not the start of a game but the launch of an attack. But in these publications – which were even produced in prisoner-of-war or internment camps and, notably, by the Germans as well as the British – humour was always a much greater part of the mix than horror. In fact, horror was almost always kicked into the long grass, though there was always a place for gravity, and, most importantly, for grief for comrades who, in the language of the time, had 'gone west'. Out of this huge ruck *The Wipers Times* emerged as the undoubted classic, even winning the accolade of being successfully re-published in Britain while the war was still on, gaining notices – one might almost claim – to die for.

The Wipers Times, first launched in February 1916, was the brain-child of two infantry officers who'd been in the thick of things ever since the Battle of Loos in 1915 and knew what the war was about. Moreover, it should be noted, they came not from some smart battalion with a tradition drawn from the public schools or the older universities, but from a rugged unfashionable regiment of the north midlands, the Notts and Derbys, of which their unit was, in pecking order terms, virtually the lowest of the low. Captain (later Colonel) F. J. 'Fred' Roberts and his assistant, Lieutenant (later Major) J. H. Pearson, were officers of a so-called 'pioneer' battalion, the basic function of which was to provide the army with a steady supply of horny-handed, muscular, no-nonsense, do-anything labourers. In this case they were largely Nottinghamshire miners, the one romantic element in their nomenclature being that their battalion was called the 12th Sherwood Foresters, more generally known as the 12th 'Robin Hoods'. Despite this lack of social cachet the two editors were top-notch soldiers: Roberts won an MC and became Commanding Officer of his battalion; Pearson collected an MC and a DSO. As for the men in their unit, they soon acquired defter skills than those required by the pick, shovel and rifle; they became the magazine's printers – a point clearly underlined by the fact that when after the 1918 Armistice the nation's miners were instantly repatriated to work the pits back home, the publication folded overnight.

Roberts and Pearson launched *The Wipers Times* not out of a sense of high cultural duty or deep moral purpose but, much more simply, because they found an abandoned printing press somewhere in the ruins of the Belgian city of Ypres (at that time frequently referred to as Wipers), 'acquired' it in the absence of other claimants and decided then and there to make a magazine with it: surely one of the most inspired cases of looting in the First World War. They were not trained writers or journalists; in fact they were both mining engineers, who somehow saw a remarkable opportunity and went for it. They enrolled a range of contributors, one or two of whom, such as Gilbert Frankau, went on to win distinguished later careers. But they largely took on the burden of filling the pages and closing up the gaps themselves. And they did so with panache, gusto and enthusiasm, managing to maintain their high spirits through the year of the Somme, 1916, the year of Passchendaele, 1917, and the most challenging year of all in terms of battles waged and casualties lost, 1918, emerging with the confidence that they had done the best they could for the nation's cause.

Their genius was to touch the right kind of nerve, to make the connections that produced instant recognition from their intended readers. Thus they railed, to anticipate Siegfried Sassoon's telling phrase, at 'scarlet majors at the base', i.e. those shining ones who gained gongs while being well away from the action, at scrimshankers, leadswingers, men of military age who held back for any reason, including that of conscience, and they praised the P.B.I., the 'Poor Bloody Infantry', and all those who were prepared to soldier on through thick and thin. If there's one keynote poem that might be picked out from the 332 pages of *The Wipers Times* to represent the central philosophy of its creators, it would be this: the poem entitled 'Stick It', published January 1918 (printed here on page 170), by which time the war was entering its fourth year, while the magazine – by now entitled *The B.E.F. Times*, a version applicable wherever the battalion might find itself – was just about to complete its second:

> What matter though the wily Hun
> With bomb, and gas and many a gun
> In futile fury, lashes out,
> Don't wonder what it's all about –
> "Stick it." . . .

> As someone said, there's no road yet
> But had an end, your grinders set
> On this one thing, that if you grin
> And carry on, we're sure to win –
> "Stick it."

This might not be great poetry, but it was a great and necessary credo for the times.

However, this did not mean that the editors and their readers were required to venerate their military elders and betters. On the contrary, the magazine repeatedly and cheerfully mocked them. This collection's title comes from a spoof advertisement published on 31 July 1916, a month into the notoriously bloody Battle of the Somme, by which date the magazine had become, if briefly, *The Somme Times*. The doctrine emanating from the high command was that everything was going jolly well, that the British were giving the Kaiser the biff on the nose he deserved and that the enemy would be legging it back to Hunland before you could say Jack Robinson. 'ARE YOU A VICTIM TO OPTIMISM?', asked the magazine's editors, in an eye-catching half-page advertisement (see page 79). 'YOU DON'T KNOW? THEN ASK YOURSELF THE FOLLOWING QUESTIONS.' The questions were: 'Do you suffer from cheerfulness? Do you wake up in the morning feeling that all is going well for the Allies? Do you consider our leaders are competent to conduct the war to a successful issue?'

And their breezy answer was: 'We can cure you. Two days spent at our establishment will effectually eradicate all traces of it [optimism] from your system.'

The 1914-1918 war is, of course, much associated with suffering: the suffering of soldiers wounded in action; the suffering of relatives hearing of the deaths of fathers, brothers, husbands, sons; the suffering of civilians caught up in conflict in a manner that was so shockingly new at that time, now all too commonplace across the world. I think, therefore, there's a special quality about the first question listed above: '*Do you suffer from cheerfulness?*' It's a brilliant twist, a daringly witty variation on the already well-known theme. It catches the shoulder-shrugging, making-the-best-of-things, oh-what-a-lovely war attitude of the British Tommy of the Western Front, one might say, to a 'T'. It makes the central point that the best way of coping with or surviving even the ugliest aspects of modern warfare is not to let them grind you down but to grin back at them, laugh at the whole impossible situation: if you like, joke at the unjokeable. This is what *The Wipers Times,* in its twenty-three editions which ran, if with certain gaps for military reasons, until 1 December 1918, was all about, and it's this unquenchable spirit which makes this magazine the iconic work that it has now become.

What gave it its special character?

One of its hallmarks was a passion for parody. A popular poem of the time was Edward Fitzgerald's 'Rubaiyat of Omar Khayam', which, although published as far back as 1859, still had enormous appeal. *The Wipers Times,* inevitably, offered its readers 'The Rubaiyat of William Hohenzollern' (page 123), a reference to the German Kaiser whom the magazine cheerfully insulted edition after edition. (They also offered their readers, less mockingly, 'The Rubaiyat of a 'Line' Subaltern'; see page 46.) Rudyard Kipling's 'If', a national favourite today, was also hugely popular then. Almost inevitably the magazine came up with its own cleverly crafted version, of which the following are the first lines:

> If you can drink the beer the Belgians sell you,
> And pay the price they ask with ne'er a grouse,
> If you believe the tales that some will tell you,
> And live in mud with ground sheet for a house. . .

For the full version see page 147. Other parodies included a running serial by Herlock Shomes, diary entries by a Lieut. Samuel Pepys, while Hilaire Belloc was mocked as Belary Holloc and the outrageous braggart Horatio Bottomley, famous as the editor of the magazine *John Bull,* was teased as Cockles Tumley.

If there was one writer whom the editors parodied with as much anger as wit, it was the *Daily Mail* columnist W. Beach Thomas, who was regularly slagged as 'Our Special Correspondent, Mr. Teech Bomas'. His crucial fault was to make himself, not the Tommy, the hero of his despatches; look at any 'Teech Bomas' extract in the following pages and you will understand precisely what a correspondent should not do when reporting from a fighting front.

They also had a brilliant talent for mockery. They frequently teased their masters and commanders; for example, targeting such wisdoms emanating from G.H.Q. as the doctrine that the enemy should never be allowed a moment's peace, that the 'Hun' must always be kept on his toes and that the German wire was 'our front line'. In short, you must be 'offensive' at all times:

> Ne'er be peaceful, quiet, or pensive,
> "Do your best to be offensive."
> His success shall greatest be
> Who regards this homily.
> In the future day and night be
> "As offensive as you might be."

This appears on page 59: for a cartoon on the same theme, see page 58, opposite.

Features such as 'Our Matrimonial Column' (page 96) offered an even gentler way of taunting their military superiors. Hence: 'BRIG-GENERAL. – Young – charming personality – feels lonely. Bashfulness has made him take this way of settling his future happiness, and he would like to correspond with some priceless young lady, matrimonially inclined.' 'BRIG-GENERAL. Companiable [sic] – jocose – domesticated – loving. Is feeling his unattached condition very much, and seizes this opportunity of making overtures to some sympathetic young lady.' The editors were well aware that would raise a smile if not a guffaw among men whose standard image of a brigadier-general was of a glaring, heavily-moustached fire-eater charging through the trenches with a horde of red-capped, chinless staff-officers in his wake, throwing off brusque orders in all directions.

Letters to the Editor were as much part of the culture as in the pages of their more famous namesake, *The Times* of London. Mocking one of that publication's annual obsessions, the following letter appeared in the edition of 20 January 1917 (printed here on page 108):

Sir,

As I was going over the top last week I distinctly heard the call of the cuckoo. I claim to be the first to have heard it this spring, and should like to know if any of your readers can assert that they have heard it before me.

I am, sir.

Yours faithfully,

A LOVER OF NATURE

However, there was much serious stuff as well. *The Somme Times* of 31 July 1916 might have its usual quota of jokes, but it also included a moving poem called 'God-Speed' (reproduced on page 78), expressing the firm belief that, despite the rigour of the fighting, genuine progress was being made. These stanzas convey its flavour:

> For a year we've taken what came along,
> We've fought or worked and we've held our line,
> Till August finds us 'going strong,'
> The game's afoot and the goal's the Rhine. . . .

> We've learnt the game in a grim hard school
> Where mistakes had a price that 'twas hard to pay,
> With Death sitting by and holding the rule,
> And conducting our studies by night and day.

> But we've also learnt, and 'tis good to know,
> That the pal of a dug-out's a friend worth while,
> For friendships made 'neath the star-shell's glow
> Means 'Help every lame dog over a stile.'

Note this poem's emphasis on friendship, a crucial element in this war of the trenches: for the flip side of this watch out for the characteristic black-bordered notice commemorating the deaths of honoured comrades reproduced here on page 126; three distinguished fatalities named, but, remembered with them anonymously, 'those others who have left us lately'. These men knew that this was at all times a deadly war fought at enormous cost.

At the end, however, we find what we might see today as a curious reaction. Perhaps the most memorable Armistice Day poem is the much quoted one by Siegfried Sassoon with its striking first line: 'Everyone suddenly burst out singing.' But there were many who did not join in the general chorus, among them, it would seem, the editors of *The Wipers Times*. Instead of hats being thrown in the air at the final ceasefire, there was a hint of wistful regret at the loss of the best aspects of the long ordeal through which they had come. See the movingly elegiac paragraph in the final edition of December 1918 entitled, strikingly, 'The Horrors of Peace' (see page 189):

> We have had a good look at the horrors of war, and now we are undergoing another sort of frightfulness. What a life! Can anyone tell us of a nice war where we could get work and so save our remaining hair from an early greyness?

The frightfulness in question was the 'barrage of paper' and the surge of bureaucracy that had suddenly turned a straightforward campaign into a nightmare of red-tape and officiousness, though it is not too difficult to see this as a metaphor for the abrupt and disturbing change of agenda when an army advancing purposefully towards what promises to be a great victory is stopped dead in its tracks:

> We are taking up a defensive position in various towns, and there we are going to hold on at all costs . . . As I remarked before, if anyone knows of a *nice* war, or if one can be arranged, we hope we shall be allowed first call.

Understandably many fighting men felt disorientated at the end of the war that had dominated their lives for so long. As concentration on the present gave way to uncertainty about the future, there could be acute anxiety, even fear, as to what role they might find in a situation where their well-honed skills were no longer relevant. When we think of the world *not* fit for heroes to which so many survivors returned, with its queues of unemployed and the well-known images of ex-Tommies selling bootlaces and match-boxes on city street corners, who is to say that those anxieties were not justified? There seems no doubt that Pearson and Roberts were among those countless thousands who never again achieved the fulfilment they had found in the war of the Western Front.

There is a moving postscript to this story. When a collected edition of the magazine was published in 1930, Roberts was still on hand to continue his editorial function. By this time the version of the war that largely prevails today was already gaining acceptance, notably through the huge success of such works of disenchantment as Erich Maria Remarque's *All Quiet on the Western Front* and Robert Graves's *Goodye to All That*: other writers in similar vein, such as Siegfried Sassoon and Wilfred Owen, would soon follow. Yet Roberts had never lost his belief in the essential justice of the cause for which he had fought and deeply resented the imputation that the war in which so many had suffered or died was an exercise in culpable futility. Focusing on the grim battlefield, the Ypres Salient, which had effectively given *The Wipers Times* its title, he devised for the new edition this highly charged dedication:

TO THE SOLDIERS OF THE SALIENT
AND THE TRUTH ABOUT THE WAR

The 'truth about the war' was, clearly, *his* truth as he saw it, not the new truth now being promulgated to the disadvantage of the old.

He allowed himself one further gesture of protest. In the Foreword which he contributed to the new edition, harking back to the time of the great German attack of 21 March 1918 (the event most responsible for taking his magazine off the presses in the war's final year), he struck out at the best-selling titles now commanding the literary field in a rousing foray of *Wipers Times*-style wit:

> Hastily taking two aspirin and placing helmet, gas, in position, I looked out of the door, only to find the beautiful March morning obscured by what seemed to be one of London's best old-style November fogs. Shouting for batman, Adjutant, Sergeant, Sergeant-Major and the Mess-Waiter, I emerged into the chilly air, which was being torn and rent in the most alarming way. All was *not* quiet on the Western Front, the Sub-Editor and I drank a case of whiskey, shot the Padre for cowardice and said "good–bye to all that". (The influence of these modern War Books is most insidious.)

And after that he disappeared, eventually resuming his pre-war career as a mining prospector, dying in obscurity in Canada in 1964. Yet his and his comrade's work has survived, not by chance but because it had to, as an essential element in the fabric of the First World War, an element necessary to its understanding.

The year 2006 saw the republication of the collected *Wipers Times* in a handsome, finely printed edition, its dust-jacket subtly aged as if to suggest that copies might have stood on the shelves of a gentleman's club or in the library of a country house of the inter-war years. (Perhaps Colonel Mustard was reading one when he was hit over the head with the fatal candlestick!) Its success was such that the publishers have decided to offer a choice selection in a reduced format, which, if not quite hip-flask in size, is arguably fitter for reading in the train, the bus or the plane, or for browsing in bed without fear of its falling uncomfortably on the reader's nose. Hence this – we hope – concise, companionable volume. As for the matter of the selection of what appears in these pages, there was no scientific process; think rather of an extra-large box of high-quality chocolates from which handfuls of favourites have been scooped to fill a smaller container. Anyone else's choice would have been equally valid, such is the richness of the original collection.

To conclude: laughter and mockery and poking fun at authority have been part of the warp and weft of the British military psyche for centuries and it was singularly unlikely that so great a comic tradition would have nothing to say about the new circumstances of 1914-1918, however challenging they might seem. Came the danger, came the leg-pulls, the quips, the spoofs and the jokes. Came the suffering, came the cheerfulness. The outcome was a brilliant philosophy for the time, a philosophy to get men through everything, or almost everything, that the war could throw at them.

Which is why I believe that this modest volume can be claimed, in its way, as virtually as important a statement about that almost hundred-years-old war as the official histories, the massive biographies, the scholarly analyses. Its spirited, vibrant voice is one that should be heard.

Enjoy!

Malcolm Brown

Captain Fred Roberts, the editor of *The Wipers Times*

GLOSSARY

A key to some of the names, terms and phrases used in *The Wipers Times*. (See also the magazine's own selection on pages 113-15.)

B.E.F. British Expeditionary Force; the British Army in France

Bill Short for Kaiser Bill, or Kaiser Wilhelm, i.e. the German Emperor, the British soldiers' arch bogey-man

Blighty England, Home and Beauty, from a Hindustani word meaning a foreign country

A 'Blighty' Alternatively a 'Blighty one'; a wound severe enough to get a soldier back home, but not bad enough to disable or kill

Bosch, Bosche The Germans; also known as Huns, Fritz or Jerry

Brass Hats General and Senior Staff Officers, the nickname due to their caps gleaming with gold lace

Bully, or tin of bully Corned beef, a staple diet of the trench war

C.O. Commanding Officer

Cloth Hall The great building in the Market Square at Ypres which became the city's most famous ruin

Cox The name of the bank used by British soldiers

C.T. Communication trench; a trench running from the rear to the front line

Division The organisation consisting of 12,000 to 20,000 men in which soldiers lived, breathed and were moved about the front

Duckboard Wooden device for providing floors for trenches or tracks across wet or marshy ground

Estaminet French or Belgian pub providing flat beer and modest white wine

F.P. 1 Field Punishment No 1; a much resented British practice whereby soldiers found guilty of some misdemeanour were strapped to a gunwheel or similar object

Flammenwerfer A German flame-thrower; a much hated weapon

G.H.Q. General Headquarters; somewhere far off, remote, another world

Haig Field Marshal Sir Douglas Haig, the British commander-in-chief from December 1916

'In the pink' In good order: term frequently used in letters home to let the family know a soldier was in sound health

Kultur Meaning German culture; not a concept that endeared itself to the men of the B.E.F.

Little Willie Popular name for the Kaiser's son, Crown Prince Wilhelm, himself a serving field commander

Minnie Jokey name for the Minenwerfer, a German trench mortar

M.O. Medical Officer

Napoo Adaptation of French 'il n'y a plus', meaning 'no more', i.e. gone, finished, non-existent

No Man's Land The dangerous, much contested area between opposing trenches

Offensive A large-scale attack; also an attitude of mind which soldiers were supposed to have at all times

Over the top To go 'over the top' was to climb over the parapet to attack the enemy

P.B.I. Poor Bloody Infantry: the term included officers as well as men

Pop Poperinghe, the Belgian town west of Ypres which provided the railhead to the Ypres Salient

Q.M. Quartermaster; the NCO responsible for providing food and clothing

R.A.M.C. Royal Army Medical Corps

R.S.M. Regimental Sergeant Major, to the ordinary soldier a figure of great eminence and awe

R.E. Royal Engineers

Salient, especially the Ypres Salient The notorious battleground to the east of Ypres fought over from October 1914 to October 1918

Sapper An ordinary soldier of the Royal Engineers

Sausage A sausage-shaped observation balloon

Staff-officers Very necessary for purposes of organisation, but hated because they worked behind the lines, were always impeccably dressed and were thought to look down on the men doing the actual fighting

Strafe To fire upon with rifles or artillery; also a noun meaning a burst of rifle or artillery fire

Subaltern A junior officer: a first or second lieutenant

Tommy Popular name for the British soldier, but not a name popular with British soldiers.

Trench feet A painful condition acquired by standing around too long in wet trenches

Verdun A city in eastern France, focus of a ferocious battle in 1916

W.A.A.C. Women's Auxiliary Army Corps, formed in February 1917 or a member of the same: to the soldiers of the war's last phase a vision of rare beauty

Whizz-bang A light shell fired from smaller field artillery guns: the name is descriptive of its actual sound

Wind up Fear; sometimes also known as wind vertical

Wipers A wartime name for Ypres, which caught on rapidly in 1914 and was very popular with the British press, though ordinary soldiers tended to use simpler versions such as 'Eepray' or 'Eeps'

Zero Zero Hour: the appointed time for an attack

◎ T H E ◎
WIPERS TIMES.
OR
SALIENT NEWS.

Editorial.

Having managed to pick up a printing oufit (slightly soiled) at a reasonable price, we have decided to produce a paper. There is much that we would like to say in it, but the shadow of censorship enveloping us causes us to refer to the war, which we hear is taking place in Enrope, in a cautious manner. We must apoiogise to our sucscribers for the delay in going to press. This has been due to the fact that we have had many unwelcome visitors near our print-ing works during the last few days, also to the difficulty of obtaining an overdraft at the local bank. Any little short-comings in production must be excused on the grounds of inexperience and the fact that pieces of metal of various sizes had punctured our press. We hope to publish the " Times " weekly, but should our effort come to an untimely end by any adverse criticism or attentions by our local rival, Messrs. Hun and Co., we shall consider it an unfriendly act, and take steps accordingly. We take this opportunity of stating that we accept no responsibiliiy for the statements in our advertisements. In conclusion we must thank those outside our salaried staff who have contributed to this, our first issue, and offer our condolences to those who have paid 20 francs for a copy. The latter will at least have the comfort of knowing that proceeds have gone to a worthy cause.

The EDITOR.

The Editor takes no responsibility for the views expressed, or the thirst for information on the part of our sub-scribers.

Reflections on Being Lost in Ypres at 3 a.m.

I wish I had been more studious as a youth. Then I should not have neglected the subjects I disliked. Then I should not have failed to cultivate the sense of geography. And thus I should not have contrived to lose myself so often in Ypres in the small hours of winter mornings.

Lost in Ypres. It is an eerie experience. Not a soul to be seen not a voice to be heard. Only far out on the road to Hooge, the quick impulsive rattle of the British machine guns answers the slower more calculating throbbing of the Hun variety. If a man would understand what hate means, let him wander along the Menin Road in the evening, and then let him find some poet, or pioneer, or artilleryman to express what he feels concerning the Hun operator in that concrete machine-gun redoubt.

Lost in Ypres at night: in the daytime it is a difficult feat to accomplish Transports and troops pass and re-pass along the ruined streets. From almost every aspect, through gigantic holes torn in the intervening walls, the rugged spikes of the ruined cathedral town mark the centre of the town. From time to time, too, the heavy thud of a " crump," (like some old and portly body falling through a too frail chair with a crash to the floor), is an unerring guide to the main square.

But at night all is different. The town is well-nigh deserted. All its inhabitants, like moles, have come out at dusk and have gone, pioneers and engineers, to their work in the line. Night after night they pass through dangerous ways to more dangerous work. Lightly singing some catchy chorus they move to and fro across the open road, in front of the firing line, or hovering like black ghosts, about the communication trenches, as if there were no such thing as war. The whole scene lights up in quick succession round the semi-circle of the salient as the cold relentless star-shells sail up into the sky. Here and there, a " grouser " airs his views, but receives little sympathy, for the men are bent on their work, and do it with a will.

All this while, however, I have been standing lost in Ypres. I cannot steer by the star-shells, for they seem to be on every side. And at night, too, the jagged spires of the cathedral are reduplicated by the remains of buildings all over the city. Like the fingers of ghosts they seem to point importunately to heaven, crying for vengeance. It is a city of ghosts, the city of the dead. For it and with it the sons of three nations have suffered and died. Yet within that city, not many days ago, a little maid of Flanders was found playing. That is an omen. Ypres has died, but shall live again. Her name in the past was linked with kings ; but to-morrow she will have a nobler fame. Men will speak of her as the home of the British soldier who lives in her mighty rampart caverns or in the many cellars of her mansions. And even when the busy hum of everyday life shall have resumed its sway in future days, still there will be heard in ghostly echo the muffled rumbling of the transport, and the rhythmic tread of soldiers' feet.

By " THE PADRE."

◁O▷

EDITOR

SUB-EDITOR

People We Take Our Hats Off To.

—o—

The person who re-introduced the sale of whisky in Pop.

The gallant C.O. who has just got his Brigade.

The officer in charge of the costume department of the Fancies.

The person who introduced the order forbidding Company Commanders to go beyond their front line trench.

The Editor of this earnest periodical. (Thank you SO much. ED.)

Things We Want To Know.

The name of the brunette infantry officer whose man got hold of the carrier pigeons, (sent to this celebrated Company Commander when his communications in the front line had broken down) and cooked them. Also who were his guests?

—o—

The name of the M.O. who attended one of the leading lights of the Fancies, and was overcome by her many charms.

—o—

The celebrated infantry officer who appears daily in the trenches disguised as a Xmas tree.

—o—

Why the dug-out of a certain Big Man is so much affected by subalterns of tender years, and if this has anything to do with the decorations on his walls.

—o—

The weekly wage bill at the Fancies.

R. B.

Agony Colnmn.

E J. N. and L. S. P. Meet us at the Clock, Popperinghe Station, at 6 p.m. Wear red carnations, so that we shall know you.—Plymouth.

WILL any patriotic person please lend a yacht and L10,000 to a lover of peace. Size of yacht immaterial.—Address Lonely Soldier, c/o Editor, Wipers.

WILL anyone lend Car to gentleman impoverished by the war. Rolls Royce preferred —Address Mishap, P.O., Box 21, Hooge.

FOR SALE, cheap, Desirable Residence. Climate warm, fine view. Splendid links close by, good shooting Terms moderate Owner going abroad.—Apply Feddup, Gordon Farm, nr Wipers.

DEAREST, I waited two hours on the Menin Road last night but you didn't come. Can it be a puncture that delayed you?—Write c/o this paper.

Occasional Notes.

—:o:—

We regret to report a further rise in property to-day.

—:o:—

The culinary department at the Hotel des Ramparts is temporarily out of action, and the emergency kitchen is in use. This should not deter intending guests from putting up at this fine old hostelry, as the prices are as heretofore, and no new cooks were necessary as a result of the accident.

—:o:—

May we ask how it is that street noises are becoming a bigger nuisance daily Several noted residents have complained that their rest is seriously interfered with. We should like to see this nuisance put a stop to immediately.

—:o:—

It has been reported to us that there is a crack visible in the cathedral spire. We should like to start a subscription list to have this repaired. Will some well-wisher head the list?

Correspondence.

—:o:—

To the Editor,
Wipers Times "

Sir,

As the father of a large family, and having two sons serving in the Tooting Bec Citizens' Brigade, may I draw your attention to the danger from Zeppelins. Cannot our authorities deal with this menace in a more workmanlike way. My boys, who are well versed in military affairs, suggest a high barbed wire entanglement being erected round the British Isles. Surely something can be done :—

PATER FAMILIAS.

—o—

To the Editor,
" B.E.F. Times."

Sir,

The other evening while taking a stroll through the system of canals which festoon the district, I called at the local soup kitchen, thinking that a cup of hot refreshing soup would compensate me for having missed my evening tot of rum. I was here met with a query as to how a perspiring and angry individual could " Supply the bloomin' Harmy wi' soup, when all he could find was a couple er dead Huns, and well scraped bone, and turnip tops? " Can nothing be done ?

INDIGNANS.

—o—

To the Editor.

Sir,

May I through the medium of your valuable paper call attention to the disgraceful state of repair the roads are getting into. What, what I ask are our city fathers doing to allow such a state of things to come to pass.

Hoping you will give this letter the publicity that I consider it merits.

I am a
WELL WISHER.

—o—o—o—

To the Editor,
" B.E.F. Times."

Sir,

I am a brain worker to whom peace and quiet are a necessity. After moving my quarters many times, I, at length, found a district which seemed to possess those advantages. I WAS MISTAKEN. Shortly after taking up my residence here a " lady " (of whose character the less said perhaps the better) has come to live opposite my house. I am no moralist, but I must protest against the noises in the street caused either by the " lady " herself or by persons interested in her. The " lady " I believe is known as "Minnie," Can nothing be done to move, or at least to have her kept quiet ?

I am, sir,
Yours Faithfully,
" PAX."

—o—o—o—

The world wasn't made in a day;
And Eve didn't ride on a 'bus, .
But most of the world's in a sandbag
The rest of it's plastered on us,

Stop Press News.

As we go to press we hear from our esteemed contemporary the "D.C.C." that a German was seen in 1 4 B 2-1 . wearing red braces, this is awful.

Addition to " People We Take Our Hats Off To " The R.B.

Our original estimate of day of publication was rather optimistic. As a certain liveliness has delayed us, for this and the errors made in our haste we apologise.

OUR NEW SERIAL.

Herlock Shomes at it Again.

SHOT IN THE CULVERT.

CHARACTERS :

BILL BANKS—A Corpse.

LIZZIE JONES—A Questionable. Person Living at Hooge.

HAROLD FITZ GIBBONS—Squire of White Chateau, (in love with Honoria.)

INTHA PINK—A Pioneer (in love with himself).

HONORIA CLARENCEAUX—The Heroine, (in love with Pink).

HERLOCK SHOMES.

DR. HOTSAM, R.A.M.C.

CHAPTER 1.

The wind was howling round the rugged spires of the Cloth Hall, and the moon shone down on the carriage bringing the elite of the old town to the festivities arranged to celebrate the 73rd term of office of Jacques Hallaert, the venerable mayor of Typers. Also the same moon shone down on the stalwart form of Intha Pink, the pioneer. He sighed as he passed the ' brilliantly lighted scene of festivity, thinking of days gone by and all that he had 'lost. As he plodded his way, clad in gum. boots, thigh, pairs one, he soliloquised aloud thus :—" What a blooming gime ! They gives me a blooming nail, they gives me a blooming 'ammer, and then they tells me to go and build a blooming dug-out." At that moment Intha fell into a crump-hole, and then continued his soliloquies thus :

{To be Continued.}

Editorial.

As our previous issue was so well received by the public, we hasten to produce our second number. At the last moment (by the payment of an enormous sum of money) we were able to secure the services of Winifred Honey-Saxwell, the well-known serial writer. Also we propose to make an effort to secure articles from other well-known writers. Of course the production of a high-class journal of this nature means enormous expense, but we do not mind that if our efforts meet with success. We are hopeful of getting articles from Bellary Helloc, and Cockles Tumley, but may not receive them in time for this number. Also Major Taude has promised to send us his views on the situation. These will be useful, We hear that Messrs. Hun and Co. are claiming a larger circulation than ourselves. This is false, and we are prepared to place our figures before any chosen tribunal. For the benefit of the public we now state that our figures are :—

Copies printed — 100
Disposed of — 100
Returned — NIL

and we now challenge any other paper in Wipers to beat our circulation.

We also wish to draw the attention of the public to our " Insurance scheme." Full particulars will be found on Page 4 of the present issue. This scheme entails vast expense for us, but we do not mind that, as the one object of our existence is to help the public. Who drew your attention to the disgraceful state of the roads, and the crack in the Cathedral spire and many other evils ? Buy the paper that tells you the truth ! All others are rotten, and the truth is not in them. We have raised the nominal price of the paper to 100 francs for appearance sake only. However, we are very grateful for the subscriptions to hand, and "THE PADRE's" Charity will benefit accordingly.

THE EDITOR.

People We Take Our Hats off To.

——:o:——

9th Royal Sussex.

Things We Want to Know.

——:0:——

1.—Whe discovered the salient.

—o—

2.—Why.

—o—

3.—Whether the "Christmas tree" expert mentioned last week is not likely to have a rival shortly.

—o—

4.—And if a pretty competition is likely to be seen.

Answers

to Correspondents.

——o—o—o——

ETHEL.—No, we have none of Kirschner's pictures in our editorial sanctum This austere chamber still retains it's scheme of simplicity. (But if you have any we have a friend whose views are not our own, who might like them.)

—:o:—

S. LACKER.—We read your letter with much interest. We fully appreciate the many difficulties which beset your path, and thus deprive the country of your services. We know how hard it is to decide between two obvious duties, and must commend your fortitude in having chosen the harder part.

—:o:—

OVIUM.—We have found that hens lay better if their exertions remain un disturbed. The ideal place you mention to encourage industry on the part of your poultry would be difficult to find. The best we can suggest is that you establish a poultry farm at Hooge or neighbourhood. Here at least your hens would have a counter excitement which we have always found is a great inducement.

—:o:—

WORRIED.—In affairs of the heart we should advise you to write direct to Sylvia, who will deal with all these knotty problems in our next issue.

OUR GREAT INSURANCE SCHEME.

NSURE AT ONCE BY PLACING AN ORDER FOR THIS PAPER WITH YOUR NEWSAGENT

Why face the awful danger of submarine

Without being Insured. 10,000,000 (ten million), has been subscribed at the local bank to carry out the largest Insurance Scheme instituted by any paper.

In the event of death caused by a submarine, anywhere in the Wipers district, your next of kin will be entitled to claim 11s. 7d., if you had at the time of death, one of our coupons fully-signed, and bearing name of Newsagent.

PLACE YOUR ORDER AT ONCE TO AVOID DISAPPOINTMENT !!!

By Belary Helloc.

In this article I wish to show plainly that under existing conditions, everything points to a speedy dis integration of the enemy We will take first of all the effect of war on the male population of Germany. Firstly, let us take as our figures, 12,000,000 as the total fighting population of Germany Of these 8,000,000 are killed or being killed hence we have 4,000,000 remaining. Of these 1,000,000 are non-combatants. being in the Navy. Of the 3,000,000 remaining, we can write off 2,500,000 as tempermentally unsuitable for fighting, owing to obesity and other ailments engendered by a gross mode of living This leaves us 500 000 as the full strength. Of these 497,250 are known to be suffering from incurable diseases, thus leaves us 2,750 Of these 2 150 are on the Eastern Front, and of the remaining 600, 584 are Generals and Staff.

Thus we find that there are 16 men on the Western Front. This number I maintain is not enough to give them even a fair chance of resisting four more big pushes, and hence the collapse of the Western Campaign. I will tell you next week about the others, and how to settle them

Stop-gap.

—:0:—

Little stacks of sandbags,
Little lumps of clay :
Make our blooming trenches,
In which we work and play.

Merry little whizz-bang,
Jolly little crump ;
Made our trench a picture,
Wiggle, woggle, wump.

Correspondence.

—:o:—

To the Editor,
   "Wipers Times."

Sir,
   May I draw your attention to the fact that the gas mains of the town seriously need attention. I was returning from the Cloth Hall Cinema the other night, when a big leak broke out in the Rue de Lille; and it was only by promptly donning my helmet-gas, that I was able to proceed on my way.

   I am, etc.,
      A LOVER OF FRESH AIR

—:o:—

To the Editor.

Sir,
   On taking my usual morning walk this morning, I noticed that a portion of the road is still up. To my knowledge the road has been in this state of repair for at least six months. Surely the employees of the Ypres Corporation can do better than this.

   I am,
      EARLY RISER.

—:o:—

To the Editor.

Sir,—Whilst walking along the Rue de Lille the other night, a gentleman (sic) coming in the opposite direction accosted me quite abruptly with the words " Who are you ? " When I told him not to be inquisitive he became quite offensive, and assumed a threatening attitude. This incident was repeated several times before I had reached the Square. I endeavoured to find a constable, but could not. Where are our police, and what are they doing? Have any more readers had the similar unpleasant experience o

   Yours, etc.,
      TIMIDITY.

War.

—:o:—

Take a wilderness of ruin,
Spread with mud quite six feet deep;
In this mud now cut some channels,
Then you have the line we keep.

Now you get some wire that's spiky,
Throw it round outside your line,
Get some pickets, drive in tightly,
And round these your wire entwine.

Get a lot of Huns and plant them,
In a ditch across the way;
Now you have war in the making,
As waged here from day to day.

Early morn the same old "stand to"
Daylight, sniping in full swing;
Forenoon, just the merry whizz-bang.
Mid-day oft a truce doth bring.

Afternoon repeats the morning,
Evening falls then work begins;
Each works in his muddy furrow,
Set with boards to catch your shins.

Choc a block with working parties,
Or with rations coming up;
Four hours scramble, then to dug-out,
Mud-encased, yet keen to sup.

Oft we're told "Remember Belgium,"
In the years that are to be;
Crosses set by all her ditches,
Are our pledge of memory.

By a Visitor.

—o—o—o—

If you happen to be a fortunate visitor to Ypres in these energetic times, there is much to see and learn for those who move about with their eyes open. By a fortunate visitor I mean when you chance to arrive on one of the quiet days —days when the number of shells sent in by the Hun does not exceed 100 per hour (meal times excepted)—you are then able to move about in comparative safety. As a visitor one tries naturally to imagine something of what the historic old town looked like before modern artillery began to destroy the work of hundreds of years, and although one can see all these ruins of buildings, note the terrific effect of shell fire on walls many feet thick, one somehow feels how impossible it is to describe what Ypres looks like, one has to see it to understand the awful dead, forsaken appearance of the place. Then if your visit has brought you up at a time when the old town is lighted up by a full moon, and you happen to be of a somewhat sentimental turn of mind, you will find yourself marvelling at the wondrous beauty of the ruined city, somehow the odd spires, broken towers, fragments of massive walls, fronts of demolished houses all have their rough jagged edges softened by the moonlight, and from these thoughts it is but a step to go on and try to reason out the why and wherefore of these things. One is almost tempted to doubt if there is an over-ruling Power for Good in this world in which we live, and to attempt to reason that no possible good can come out of such appalling misery and desolation; but surely this is another case of the finite mind coming into contact with the Infinite? Then listen! away to the east a faint whistle through the air, then another, coming this way—an explosion, and the guide says—"They're shelling Hell-Fire Corner again," then quiet again, and later on as you wonder across the Square, you see the motor ambulances wending their way back to Pop. with their loads of mauled humanity, somebody's loved ones, to be looked after and tended by skilled hands—with no effort spared to alleviate pain and repair the damage—and as you travel home you will have many things to remember and think about—after your visit to Ypres,

ONE WHO IS NOT "A PADRE,"

Sporting Notes

The Spring Handicap, was run for on the Hooge Course last Wednesday, and the sport was all that one could desire. The course being in rare condition—as stated in our last number—and the candidates trained to an ounce. The locally-trained animal "East Wind" just managed to catch the judge's eye first, but the much fancied "Chlorine" fell at the Culvert. The greatly advertised continental candidate "Fritz" look fright at the "gate," and so figures amongst the "also ran." "Whizz-bang" who was intended to make the running for "Fritz" started off at a great pace, but soon shot his bolt. "H.E." then took the lead but was audibly broken before the distance was reached. "Tommy" and "East Wind" soon had "Frost" cold, and they went on to finish an exciting race, "East Wind" winning, as previously stated, by a nosecap.

Stop Press News.

3.30 HOOGE.

Whizz-bang	1
H.E.	2

Others fell. 8 runners.

The crack is widening in the cathedral spire. Steps must be taken.

Mr. Krump has arrived in town.

4 p.m. Question asked in the House, by Mr. Toothwaite, as to what measures had been taken to stop the war. Mr. Pennant answered "Tape Measures." (Loud Cheering.)

Things We Want to Know.

—o—o—o—

The name of the Brig. Major, who, in relief orders, mentioned that one battalion of a famous regiment would find billets in three houses in Street Verbod te Wateren.

* * *

The name of the red trimmed officer who has a penchant for 5A.

* * *

The name of the Major who capitulated to the dark-eyed Belgique at the "Chateau."

* * *

Whether the bridges at a certain place are to entice the Bosche to the wire, or the wire to prevent us using the bridges.

* * *

What is Zero.

* * *

Why no steps are taken to stop the enemy, seen by a sapper officer, working behind our lines.

* * *

Whether the strong point at C2 should not have another letter in front of it.

* * *

The name of the M G.O. who has come to the conclusion that the only reason the Hun planes visit Pop. is to bomb his camp. (The personelle of which, we believe, is three N.C.O.'s and one private.)

* * *

Are we as OFFENSIVE as we might be.

"Now this 'ere" war, the corp'rl said,
    Has lasted long enuff'"
"Gorblime," said the private with
    His voice exceeding gruff,
"Not 'arf it aint !" and drew his nose
    Across his sheepskin cuff.

Urgent or Ordinary.

—o—o—o—

There was a time when first I donned the
        Khaki—
Oh, martial days in Brighton-by-the-
        Sea !—
When not the deepest draught of Omar's
        Saki
Could fire my ardent soul like dixie tea.
I dreamed of bloody spurs and bloodier
        sabre,
    Of mentions—not too modest—in
        despatches ;
I threw my foes, as Scotchmen toss the
        caber,
And sent my prisoners home in wholesale
        batches ;
Led my platoons to storm the Prussian
        trenches,
Galloped my guns to enfilade his flank ;
Was it H.M.'s own royal hand, or
        French's,
That pinned the V.C. on my tunic ?
        SWANK !
Those dreams are dead : now in my
        Wiper's dug-out,
I only dream of Kirchner's naughtiest
        chromo ;
The brasier smokes ; no window lets the
        fug out ;
And the Bosche shells ; and 'Q' still
        issues bromo.
    "For information "—" Urgent "—
        " Confidential "—
    " Secret "—" For necessary action,
        please "—
" The G.O.C. considers it essential "—
My soldier-soul must steel itself to these ;
Must face, by dawn's dim light. by
        night's dull taper,
Disciplined, dour, gas-helmeted, and
        stern,
Brigades, battalions, batteries, of paper,—
The loud 'report,' the treacherous
        return,'
Division orders, billeting epistles,
Barbed 'Zeppelin' wires that baffle
        G.H.Q.,
And the dread ' Summary ' whose blurred
        page bristles
With ' facts ' no German general ever
        knew.
Let the Hun hate ! WE need no beer-
        roused passions
To keep our sword-blade bright, our
        powder dry,

The while we chase October's o'erdrawn
rations
And hunt that missing pair of ' Gum-
boots, thigh.'

GILBERT FRANKAU.

2/3/16.

Answers

to Correspondents.

—o—o—o—

COMMERCE, YPRES.—We are very much
afraid that the County Council will
refuse you a street hawking licence—
still there is no harm in applying for
one.

—:o:—

GRATEFUL READER.—Bravo !—Glad you
like the paper. Yours is one of the
countless homes we have brought a
little sunshine into.

—:o:—

X.Y.Z., ZERO, AUNTY and others will be
answered in due course.

The privit to the sergeant said
" I wants my blooming rum."
" Na poo," the sergeant curtly said,
And sucked his jammy thumb.
" There's 'soup in loo' for you to-night."
The privit said, " By gum !"

LOVE AND WAR.

—o—o—o—

In the line a soldiers's fancy
Oft may turn to thoughts of love.
But too hard to dream of Nancy
When the whizz-bangs sing above.

—§ † §—

In the midst of some sweet picture.
Vision of a love swept mind,
Bang ! " A whizz-bang almost nicked
yer ! "
" Duck, yer blighter, are yer blind ? "

—§ † §—

Take the case of poor Bill 'Arris
Deep in love with Rosy Greet,
So forgot to grease his tootsies,
Stayed outside and got " trench feet."

—§ † §—

Then remember old Tom Stoner,
Ponder on his awful fate.
Always writing to his Donah,
Lost his rum 'cos 'e was late.

—§ † §—

Then again there's 'Arry 'Awkins,
Stopped to dream at Gordon Farm.
Got a " blightie " found his Polly
Walking out on Johnson's arm.

—§ † §—

Plenty more of such examples
I could give, had I but time.
War on tender feelings tramples,
H.E. breaks up thoughts sublime.

—§ † §—

" Don't dream when you're near machine
guns ! "
Is a thing to bear in mind.
Think of love when not between Huns,
A sniper's quick, and love is blind.

A DWELLER IN WIPERS' ELEGY TO THAT TOWN.

—o—o—o—

(With apologies to Grey.)

A six-inch tolls the knell of parting
day.
The transport cart winds slowly o'er the
lea.
A sapper homeward plods his weary
way,
And leaves the world to Wipers and to
me.

—§ † §—

Now fades the glimmering star shell from
the sight,
And all the air a solemn stillness holds;
Save where a whizz-bang howls it's rapid
flight,
And "five rounds rapid" fill the distant
folds.

—§ † §—

Beneath the Ramparts old and grim and
grey,
In earthy sap, and casement cool and
deep;
Each in his canvas cubicle and bay,
The men condemned to Wipers soundly
sleep.

—§ † §—

Full many a man will venture out by
day,
Deceived by what he thinks a quiet
spell;
Till to a crump he nearly falls a prey,
And into neighbouring cellar bolts like
hell.

—§ † §—

A burning mountain belching forth it's
fire,
A sandstorm in the desert in full fling;
Or Hades with it's lid prised off entire,
Is naught to dear old Wipers in the
Spring.

Sporting Notes.

Owing to the frightful state of the ground during the last fortnight, practically all types of sport have had to be suspended. This is the long arm of coincidence as we have no more space in this number.

Our Hero's Troubles

Sketch by "Peter"   Engraver, Sapper
E. J. Couzens, R.E.

Pioneer (soliliquizes):—"They gives us a —— nail, they gives us a —— hammer, and they tells us to go and build a —— dug-out."

STOP! STOP!! STOP!!!

NOW THAT SPRING IS COMING

YOU REQUIRE SHADE.

WE ARE IN A POSITION TO OFFER THE PUBLIC

250,000,000 SAPLINGS

OF THAT FULSOME, PROLIFIC AND UMBRAGEOUS PLANT,

THE POPLAR

—o—o—o—o—

WHAT ARE YOU GOING TO HANG THAT HAMMMOCK ON?

—SURELY NOT THE FISH HOOK—

Therefore Buy While Opportunity Offers.

—o—o—o—o—

OLD WORLD AVENUES A SPECIALITY.

—o—o—o—o—

ADDRESS: FILL, POTS & Co. RENINGHELST.

EDITORIAL.

This week we have the pleasure to place before our readers the first number of Volume 2. Also we publish herewith a balance sheet :—

	FRANCS.
Subscriptions received	395
Already given to the PADRE'S Charity	225
Balance in hand	170
	395

Our subscription list has grown to an alarming extent, and we much regret that we have been unable to supply all who have sent for copies. Our new machine has given the greatest satisfaction in every way, and has fully warranted the enormous amount outlaid. Mr. BELARY HELLOC has unfortunately caught a cold while attending an outdoor meeting of his constituents at Hooge, and is consequently confined to bed in his luxurious suite of apartments at the Hotel des Ramparts. Our reporter interviewed him with a request for an article, but he was only well enough to reply " Getterlongoutervit." However, Mr. COCKLES TUMLEY was run to ground in Oxford Street, and promised to weigh in with an article after he had attended a meeting of his creditors at the Cloth Hall. Still the City Fathers neglect our repeated warnings, and in the election next week Mr. SHEMBERTONS WILLING, who is fighting the constituency on the " Better Lighting " platform, will put up a winning fight against the absurd addle-pated policy of those effete wrecks who sit in the Corporation of the City. Must we again mention that there is a crack visible in the Cathedral spire? Surely it should be obvious to anyone who has the interests of the City at heart. Is it necessary that we again draw the attention of those concerned to the fact that the buildings are encroaching on the fairway? Let us turn from this sickening spectacle of fatheaded complacency to a fairer scene. Owing to the enterprise of one who prefers anonymity, we shall be able to sit in the shade during the summer nights that are coming. Kew Gardens within a few minutes' walk of the Hotel des Ramparts! What a magnificent dream! And as we sit telling the old sweet tale in the shade of some mighty poplar, let us not forget that, but for the magnificent generosity of one who prefers to remain unknown, we might still have had to sit on the shadeless banks of the Moat. Remembering that, let us vote for SHEMBERTONS WILLING. This week we have reduced the price to 50 centimes on account of the paper famine. Many happy returns of the day!

THE EDITOR.

People We Take Our Hats off To.

—:o:—

The French.

For Exchange.

FOR EXCHANGE.—A SALIENT, in good condition. Will exchange for a PAIR of PIGEONS, or a CANARY. —Apply Lonely Soldier, Hooge.

LOST.

LOST, on Thursday night last, DIAMOND BRACELET, about 11 p.m., between the Menin Gate and Hooge. Thought to have been lost when owner was returning from the second house at the Cloth Hall. Finder will be suitably rewarded.—Mrs. I. Pink, Stables Avenue, Hooge.

SOME KNOWLEDGE.

Way back from home
Across the foam
For Hunnish blood a-thirsting,
Came Captain Bass
(As green as grass)
With knowledge simply bursting.

—§ † §—

In training days
His studious ways
Caused all to gaze in wonder,
On field days long
When all went wrong
He never seemed to blunder.

—§ † §—

Now strange to say
The very day
That Bass arrived in Flanders,
Another too
Arrived at " Q "
His name was Percy Sanders.

—§ † §—

How different he
Appeared to be
In contrast to our hero,
He did not roar
For Hunnish gore
His spirits seemed at zero.

—§ † §—

With buttons bright
And Sam Brown tight
This twain went into battle,
How happy they
Upon that day
How sweet their childish prattle.

—§ † §—

My simple lay
I grieve to say
To ghoulish taste now panders,
For you will see
That Captain " B "
Is killed and so is Sanders.

—§ † §—

Upon the ground
A dud they'd found
(It caused them stupefaction)·
In para. 3
Said Captain " B "
We'll find our course of action.

—§ † §—

It says, I see
Said Captain " B "
In fact it gives quite clearly,
With primers dry
You blow it high
Said Captain Sanders " really ! ! "

—§ † §—

It seems to me
That para. 3
Is merely futile raving,
The trouble's less
Continued " S "
To drop it on the paving.

—§ † §—

And Captain " B "
Agreed with " P "
His method seemed so clear,
They'll never more
See England's shore
They've left this mortal sphere.

TO MY CHUM.

No more we'll share the same old barn,
The same old dug-out, same old yarn,
No more a tin of bully share,
Nor split our rum by a star-shell's flare,
So long old lad.

—:o:—

What times we've had, both good and
bad,
We've shared what shelter could be had,
The same crump-hole when the whizz-
bangs shrieked,
The same old billet that always leaked,
And now—you've " stopped one."

—:o:—

We'd weathered the storm two winters
long,
We'd managed to grin when all went
wrong,
Because together we fought and fed,
Our hearts were light ; but now—you're
dead
And I am Mateless.

—:o:—

Well, old lad, here's peace to you,
And for me, well, there's my job to do,
For you and the others who lie at
rest,
Assured may be that we'll do our best
In vengeance.

—:o:—

Just one more cross by a strafed road-
side,
With it's G.R.C., and a name for guide,
But it's only myself who has lost a
friend,
And though I may fight through to the
end,
No dug-out or billet will be the same,
All pals can only be pals in name,
But we'll all carry on till the end of the
game
Because you lie there.

Military Definitions.

HOOGE	See Hell.
QUARTER MASTER or MASTER QUARTER, ONE or Q.M.	A bird of strange habits :—when attacked covers itself with indents and talks backwards.
RUM	See Warrant Officers.
DUMP	A collection of odds and ends, sometimes known as the Divisional Toyshop.
HELL , ...	See Hooge.
FOKKER	The name given by all infantry officers and men to any aeroplane that flies at a great height.
ADJUTANT ...	See grenades or birds.
INFANTRYMAN ..	An animal of weird habits, whose peculiarities have only just been discovered. It displays a strange aversion to light, and lives in holes in the earth during the day, coming out at night seeking whom it may devour. In colour it assimilates itself to the ground in which it lives.
GRENADES ...	These are used to cause annoyance to any luckless person who happens to be near them.
BIRDS	Are of two kinds only. —The Carrier Pigeon (a delicacy for front line trenches), and the nameless, untamed variety usually collected by junior officers.

Cockles Tumley.

—o—o—o—

HALT! STOP RIGHT NOW!!

—:o:—

Twenty years ago I told you what was going to happen. If I didn't I meant to. Now I'm going to ask you all to back me, I'm appealing to you, you! the independent electors of Britain. Are we going to stand it any longer? Are your women nothing to you? Brrrr!!! Are we going to put up with the business methods of Q. Why should we have business in the Army? Business must go. There! now I've said it,— BUSINESS MUST GO. Let us have no more paltry pandering to business methods. Why should we put up with the tyranny of writing pencils, carpenter, one? Let us call a spade a spade, and a "can, oil, lubricating, armourer's" an armourer's lubricating oil can. I shall be addressing meetings at Hooge, Zillebeke, and Hell Fire Corner. Roll up in your thousands, and give the lie to everybody. Who pointed out the crying need for a business trench? Brrrrrrr! Let us grasp this growing evil fearlessly and scotch it. Business in the Army! Heavens!! And we might have been caught unawares had I not warned you. How much you all owe me! Still we'll say no more of that. But now that I've warned you it's up to you. Remember that, all of you. Stop it! STOP IT!! STOP IT!!! Brrrrrrrr.

COCKLES TUMLEY.

ADIEU TO THE SALIENT.

The news is confidential ! At least, as yet, it is not known to everybody. Nevertheless it is true. Had I the vocabulary I could tell you what I think of this charming spot. Words having failed me, I bid it "Good-bye" with a silence more eloquent than words. For we are leaving the Salient and going into "rest" ! ! —

Whatever trials "rest" ? may hold, whatever the future may have for us, I think that always I shall be glad to have seen the Salient. A month there holds more than a year elsewhere, "Wipers" ! He's a strange man who can gaze on that unmoved. Who, that has known it, will forget the high-strung tension of the Menin Road, who, unmoved, can pass those fields of crosses ? The Menin Road and all it means. To know all the by-paths and alternative ways so as to dodge when shelling starts ! To know all its holes and ditches when machine guns loose ! Can there be any emotion to equal that of lying prone in a crump-hole with a machine gun ripping across your back. Hell Fire Corner ! aptly named. The span from there to Hooge, who that has slithered along it in gum boots thigh will ever forget. And now ! no more to ponder as to which route to use. No longer the old question "where are they putting 'em to-night? For we're going back to "rest" ! !

But not all—some of us remain, Poor lads : There they stay in the Salient and crosses mark the PRICE they paid. Always, when the strain of the Salient may have left us, the memory of those crosses will remain, and those true hearts who sleep there may rest assured that we, who worked with them, fought with them and hoped with them, will exact the price. Ypres, and all you mean farewell ! To those who come after us good luck ! We are going back to "rest" ! ! !

NOTICE.

We regret to announce that an insidious disease is affecting the Division, and the result is a hurricane of poetry. Subalterns have been seen with a note-book in one hand, and bombs in the other absently walking near the wire in deep communion with the muse. Even Quartermasters with books, note, one, and pencil, copying, break into song while arguing the point re boots. gum, thigh. The Editor would be obliged if a few of the poets would break into prose as a paper cannot live by "poems" alone.

Printed &
Published by
Sherwood, Forester &
Co , Ltd.
B.F. F.

THE
"NEW CHURCH" TIMES.

WITH WHICH IS INCORPOPATED

THE WIPERS TIMES

No 1. Vol 1.   Monday, 17th April, 1916.   Price 5 Francs.

EDITORIAL.

Owing to reasons over which we had no control, we regret to announce that the Wipers Times is now defunct. But through the enterprise of a wealthy syndicate all rights, plant, etc., belonging to that earnest periodical have been acquired at a fabulous figure, and are now incorporated in the new venture. Also the highly salaried staff has elected to follow the fortunes of their Editor, so that we may still hope to retain the confidence of our readers. We hope to introduce many new features shortly, including a new competition which will be open to all above the rank of Colonel. We are having a most luxurious set of offices erected, but fully believe that the incredible sums to be expended will be warranted by an increased circulation. As we have left the scene of our serial before the writer had managed to extri. cate most of the characters from the Bellewarde Bee, we shall have to tre·pass on the readers' credulity to bring some of them back, otherwise it will spoil the continuity of this enthralling tale. We have just returned from leave which is becoming a greater trial than ever. To leave this land of brightness and, by spending two hours on a Channel boat, to be placed right into an atmosphere of gloom and indef.

Initness. Oh l ye of little faith, wake up and smile for the summer is upon ye. Let your step be brisk and your hearts light for " even as ye have sown so shall ye not reap," and for that thank your lucky stars, for though ye have tried for eighteen months to lose the war yet have ye not succeeded and victory is at hand. So go ye unto the uttermost ends of darkness, yea, even unto Piccadilly and Westminster, and preach the gospel of cheeriness and hope. We notice with deep concern that the fell disease poetitis is on the increase. This may be accounted for by the arrival of Spring, and though the picture of little lambs gambolling among the whizz-bangs may be beautiful and romantic, yet our paper hungers for prose and will not be satisfied. Now we place ourselves with the utmost confidence in the hands of our readers, relying on the support so readily given to the defunct " Wipers Times."

THE EDITOR.

GOOD-BYE.

Farewell *Yperen ! Yperen farewell !
Long have I known thee, and known thee well !
Thy stoney streets, thy shell-pitted square,
Looted thy houses for dug-out ware,
Looking for cellar cool and deep,
With a shell-proof roof where I could sleep.
—§ † §—

No longer need thy ways to prowl,
With ears attuned for crump's shrill howl,
'Twixt doubtful joys to hesitate,
The Menin Road, or old Lille Gate ?
—§ † §—
But in my sleep I'll dream of thee,
And always in my thoughts thou'llt be,
Perchance my fate may be to see
Another place resembling thee,
But that foretells a future warm,
Where other little devils swarm,
Thy prototype can but be—well
Why should we mince the matter—HELL.

*Yperen—The Belgian name for Wipers, used here to baffle the enemy.

A FEW WORDS.

I read in last month's WIPERS TIMES, the Editor was sick of rhymes ; the best of reasons, I suppose, that I should henceforth stick to prose. No more I'll sing how transports wait, bi-nightly, at the Menin Gate, while some unthinking driver sits, well in effective range of Fritz—and galls his mules and smokes and spits : no more I'll turn the mordant line till ' Q ' clerks blush incarnadine ; or strafe our deadly A.S.C., in tuneful stanzas twenty three. No, never more I'll twang the lute—my Pegasus, that rope-galled brute, I'll treat as Balaam did his ass ; groom, turn the hairy out to grass !

Verse was alright when we were pent in that unkindly Salient ; but here, where April's early breeze wafts perfume over Neuve Eglise (if this takes place, I'll bet my shirt Division Signals " Gas Alert ") an easier part is mine to play

THE "NEW CHURCH" HIPPODROME.

THIS MAGNIFICENTLY EQUIPPED MUSIC HALL WILL RE OPEN ON

MONDAY NEXT.

RE-DECORATED THROUGHOUT NO EXPENSE HAVING BEEN SPARED.
COME IN YOUR HUNDREDS. STANDING ROOM FOR THOUSANDS.

GRAND CENTENARY PERFORMANCE AT WHICH

All The World-famed Artistes

WILL POSITIVELY APPEAR, INCLUDING :

WILLIAM O. N. ZOLLERN

IN HIS SCREAMINGLY FUNNY FARCE, ENTITLED

'THE BIG PUSH' 'OR OVER-DUN'

This is evidently in for a long run, and the celebrated William jun., shows all his
old irrepressability.

ETC., ETC.

| Doors open always. | Book early. | Prices as usual. |

---

for Editors who never pay.

Is it not good, dear friends, to hop away from Reninghelst and Pop ; only on others' maps to see the walls that once were Potije ; to leave the sinful whiskied throng that filled the Ramparts all night long, the snares that wait for youthful feet in City Square and Regent Street, the pit that yawns for wicked ways where Hell Fire Corner's Shell-fires blaze ; is it not good, my friends, to perch in safety by this dear new church ? For here the frisky April lamb lies down, nor cares one tinker's damn, for these our unprotected guns pointing dumb muzzles to dumb Huns : and here each happy trench is made to help the open enfilade ; and here we sleep beneath a roof which isn't even Pip-squeak proof— and e'en the WIPERS TIMES I ween, becomes a Parish Magazine.

Oh my dear friends, how sweet. how strange, this restful quiet, this peaceful change. Here let us rest while spies release with loving hands the dove of peace, that carries under wing (not beak) all knowledge our opponents seek : here let us stretch our airy wires, (remembering ' he who digs, perspires ') and hope that never hostile shell shall cut the lines we love so well.

Oh, my beloved parishoners, hark how the happy Hunlet purrs : see what a little kindliness has done to ease his frightfulness, turned into love his ravening lust and to caress his bayonet thrust.

Better is charity benign than Vickers gun and deadly mine ; better the brother love of Heaven than nine-point-two or four-point-seven !

Dear friends, with this sweet thought I close my this week's task of parish prose : may Heaven be pleased my flock to bless : . . . . yet, when in doubt, call S.O.S. !

GILBERT FRANKAU.
10/4/16.

THE EDITOR'S LAMENT.

—:o:—

Oh pity! pity! ill wind blows
My one tame poet's flown to prose,
And he on whom our hopes were based,
Whose tuneful efforts weekly graced
Our columns, has the awful taste
      To " prose it."

—:o:—

Oh! graceless churl, with scathing line
Your Editor t'incarnadine
To make his pale cheek flush with shame,
To hint at pay in lieu of fame,
And make him in despair exclaim
      I'll " Franc out."

—:o:—

And yet perchance his kindly soul
Knows not he's put me " up the pole,"
His next week's effort well may be
A gem of thought and poetry,
Which we will class eternally
      Gilbertian.

          THE EDITOR.

In dug-out cool I sit and sneeze,
Safe from a whizz-bang's mauling ;
Dreams come my appetite to tease,
Fond visions which my fancy please
Of maids divine, enthralling,
And glorious times when our job's done,
My thoughts you'll echo—" Damn the
      Hun ! "

OUR NEW SERIAL.

—o—o—o—

HERLOCK SHOLMES AT IT AGAIN.

—o—o—o—

Characters :—Same as before.

—o—o—o—

CHAPTER 5.

—o—

Snowflakes were falling heavily around Hordon Goose Farm, where we left Herlock with the fair Honoria. Breezy Bill, the Bouncing Butcher of Bellewarde, had just been hit in the neck by a whizz-bang when the chug-chug of a motor cycle was heard. "Can it be Intha?" cried Honoria, while Sholmes proceeded to tune his violin. "No !"—roared he, as a motor despatch rider came round Fell Hire Corner— "News at last from my Baker Street Squad." Hurriedly tearing open and reading the despatch, the true Sholmes stood revealed in all his strength and method. Seizing his vermoral sprayer, he rapidly squirted an enormous dose into his forearm. Just then the voice of the faithful Hotsam was heard calling "Where are you. Sholmes?" "Here" replied the great detective, rapidly emptying his revolver at the approaching figure. "Thank goodness I've found you at last, but you nearly got me that time," said Hotsam admiringly. "Never mind, better luck next time" said

Sholmes, sotto voce, to Honoria. Aloud, "To work, there's mischief afoot. Thank heaven I attended that two days course at the Technical School, I shall now be up to all their dodges." Drawing a searchlight from his pocket, he read the fateful message :—

"Division moves to-morrow at dawn AAA You will assemble all characters at zero fifteen outside Cloth Hall, Typers, P 13 D 1-1 in time to catch the underground for *——— at zero twenty AAA On arrival there steal any rations you can find, and carry on with serial AAA—EDITOR."

(* CENSORED—ED)

"At last !" shouted the great sleuth. "At last !" shouted the others, as they busily collected the usual paraphernalia of the great man. "Hotsam," cried Sholmes, "send off the orderly sergeant at once to warn all Characters. Then meet me at the Denin Gate." With these words he disappeared into the gloom and a crump-hole. All these arrangements having been made, Hotsam and Honoria continued their journey down the Denin Road, arriving in Typers just in time to meet Intha Pink before he left for his nightly work. Having rapidly given him a summary of all that had happened, they went into a neighbouring estaminet to await the fateful hour of zero.

(Another long and thrilling instalment next week.)

Correspondence.

To the Editor,
  "New Church" Times.

Sir,
On looking at some of the pictures published by the daily pictorial papers in England I am affected by a peculiar feeling of nauseau. This is especially noticeable when the subject happens to be peace meetings in Trafalgar Square, etc. Surely, if at home they must have peace meetings, and must tolerate conscientious objectors, then these might be hidden from the public eye. The only way to heal open sores is to bind them up and the ventilation of full page photos is not likely to be benefical to our best interests, besides making rather a disgusting exhibition,
  I am, Sir,
    Yours faithfully,
      A LOVER OF DECENCY.

—§ † §—

To the Editor,
  "New Church" Times.

Sir,
May I encroach upon your valuable space to draw your attention to the fact that for some days now, the clock in the tower of the church at Wulverghem, has not received the amount of attention necessary to its good running.
This fact has caused many of the workers in our little village to miss their early morning trains to Messines.
  I am, etc.,
    "TEMPUS FUGIT"

—§ † §—

RUBAIYAT OF A "LINE" SUBALTERN.

The passing whizz-bang shrieks and
    bullets hum
Yet, gentle stranger, to my dug-out
    come;
To you I'll unfold knowledge which may
    help,
But first methinks will ope a jar of rum.
—§ ⱡ §—
This is a cheery place you will allow,
A tin of beef, a jar of rum, and Thou
Beside me, squatting in a pool of mud,
And dug-out is not Paradise enow.
—§ ⱡ §—
Alas! Alas! When M.G.'s spat I swore,
I swore and swore—and then again I
    swore!—
While on my tummy lay in dank pool
    deep,
And bullets through my fav'rit breeches
    tore.
—§ † §—
And then! And then with five-nine crump
    you bet,
The wily Hun bust up our parapet,
Blew off my roof, and made that blooming
    hole,
Through which you're now so quickly
    getting wet.
—§ † §—
The surly blighter shoots, and having
    shot
Moves on, while you are cursing quite a
    lot,
And on your tummy crawl through feet
    of mud,
Nor pause till you've retaliation got.
—§ † §—
But hist! 'Tis secret known to only few,
We're going "o'er the top," and going
    through,
And then! And then! Old Fritz will
    pay in kind
The debt he owes the likes of me and you.

DUG-OUT MUSINGS.

Idly toying with a paper, something
    caught
My passing eye—
Just a picture, and the subject, can you
    guess?
A man both hale and fit,
With a touch of MOTHER WIT!
Puts his fingers to his nose and saunters
    On into his stye,
And this record left to grace the daily
    press.

Having gazed at this in wonder, then
    I sat me down to think,
And to ponder how such things had come
    to be,
Had old England changed so much
Since the years when I lost touch?
That a cur can claim attention
    While we hover on the brink,
And with effort are in sight of victory

England! What a strange digestion!
    Strain at gnats
    And swallow kine,
May we pray that you will soon shake off
    the dope,
And a cur with fingers spread
Follows where he may be led
Knowing well, that, though his conscience
    is
    Unable to define
The only way of duty, yet there's but
    one given line,
And to take it is his last remaining hope.

Answers

to Correspondents.

LOVER OF NATURE.—Nothing doing, that bird's dead.

PRO BONO.—Noise you complain of is our new metre gun. Certainly, will have it removed if it disturbs your sleep.

SUBALTERN.—No, the death penalty is not enforced in the case of murdering an adjutant, as you can always be able to prove extenuating circumstances.

YOUNG OFFICER.—It is not "the thing" to wear turned up slacks and shoes when "going over the top," in fact, you run the risk of being sent back to your unit if discovered.

TROUBLED.—Certainly think you have just complaint against people in next dug-out, and if you care to take the matter further there is no doubt that you will get damager. It certainly was scandal if, as you affirm, the picture was one of Kirschner's.

Spring is coming, watch the whizz-bang
As it shrieks with mad delight,
All the how'zers howl the message
As they break the still of night,
Through the winter, long and weary,
Cold and dreary, we have passed,
Lived and slept in Hell's own muddle,
Fed and worked in filth and puddle.
But here's end to all our worries,
Spring and sun have come at last.

The Editor would welcome articles from anyone in the Division, and would esteem it a favour if anyone knowing of buried talent would see that this is brought to light and exercised. Payment is made on the same generous lines as during the run of the "Wipers Times." So will everyone with a little spare time please dash off something and send it along.

Stop Press News.

LATEST PEACE RUMOUR.—"The Crown Prince is willing to dispose of his famous collection of valuable antiques from France and Flanders if suitable price can be obtained." The American President is writing a note about it.

Things We Want to Know.

—o—o—o—

When the sale of whisky will be introduced in Bailleul ?

—:o:—

Whether the pop'lar Poplar tree's as pop'lar as it used to be ?

—:o:—

Whether certain officers have taken shares in the Hôtel Faucon, and what's the attraction ?

—:o:—

Whether a well-known firm of commission agents isn't getting rather fed up with hurriedly changing it's quarters? (N.B.—We think this frequent sudden "flitting" might have a bad effect on this firm's custom, as the public are rather apt to fight shy of these "Here-to-day - and - gone - to-morrow" firms—verb. sap.)

—:o:—

Whether the urgent wires of a well-known C.O. (already referred to in these columns) have been more frequent during the recent hot weather ?

—:o:—

Whether one of the leaders in Kirchner collections has not got his nose in front rather by innuendo than superiority in numbers, and if the others concerned are not straining every nerve to make up leeway ?

LOST.

LOST, STOLEN, or STRAYED.—Two HUNS. Appearance, fed up and miserable. Peculiarities, hunger and a dislike of sudden noises. Mislaid somewhere in trenches at ———. Will finder please communicate with THE UMPTIETH DIVISION, Muddy Brook Alley, and he will be suitably rewarded.

OUR SHORT STORY.

Two soldiers were carrying feather mattresses up to the front line trenches when one stumbled. "Strike me pink, Bill," said one, "what's this ?" ·"A dud," said, Harry. "Ho, is it ?" said Bill, "let's see !" Picking up a maul which lay handy they saw . . . . The war went on.

EDITORIAL.

Oh, Belgium! Here in the last number we spread ourselves on themes of lovely Spring, and you, with the basest ingratitude, have turned the whole thing into a wash-out. Well! A trench without three feet of mud wouldn't seem homely anyway so perhaps you are right. This is our grand double Easter number (although the baker forgot to leave the hot-cross buns at the door) and the price is consequently doubled. We hope shortly to be able to announce the result of our "last line" Competition, but as our judging staff is at present in bed with a bad cold, caught while swimming back from the trenches the other night, all the correspondence is accumulating and the heterogeneous mass is awaiting his perusal. The sad and touching picture of a General awaiting the arrival of a D.R.L.S. announcing that he has won one of our mammoth prizes haunts us. However, there need be no anxiety, every effort will receive consideration in due time, and the prizes will go to the proper quarter. We are very glad to see that street noises are not so prevalent in our new neighbourhood, but even here there is room for improvement. We regret to state that we have been involved in a libel action over a little controversy in our columns re the premature appearance of an infernal member of the feathered tribe. This has caused us much inconvenience, but in order to exonerate ourselves in the matter we publish a resumé of the proceedings showing clearly the doubtful character of the petitioner and his associates. From the resume it can clearly be gathered that he is actuated by purely sordid financial motives, and undoubtedly, that he gained 500fr. will far outweigh the fact, that in so doing, he ventilated a mode of living which is as quesfionable as it is precarious. However, these petty nuisances happen to all papers sometime or other. We have hopes of obtaining an article from the pen of Mr. Belary Helloc on "How to win the war," but this may not arrive in time for this issue. We should welcome correspondence from readers with reference to the promotion of inter-divisional sports, etc., especially with regard to cricket. We are looking forward with pleasurable anticipation to a fine Bank Holiday, and expect to see a big throng of pleasure seekers. The rush to the sea should beat all records, and big crowds are prepared for at the international show at Verdun. Wishing you all a pleasant holiday.

THE EDITOR.

A BRACE OF GROUSE.

Two papers on a single day
Have roused my spirit to the fray.
Muse mine, my double-barrelled gun!
And let us strafe them, either one.

MINOR WORRIES.

If the Hun lets off some gas—
        Never mind.
If the Hun attacks in mass—
        Never mind.
If your dug-out's blown to bits,
Or the C.O.'s throwing fits,
Or a crump your rum jar hits—
        Never mind.

—:o:—

If your trench is mud knee-high—
        Never mind.
You can't find a spot that's dry—
        Never mind.
If a sniper has you set,
Through dents in your parapet,
And your troubles fiercer get—
        Never mind.

—:o:—

If you're whizzbanged day and night—
        Never mind.
Bully all you get to bite—
        Never mind.
If you're on a working party,
Let your grin be wide and hearty,
Though the sappers may be tarty—
        Never mind.

—:o:—

If machine guns join the muddle—
        Never mind.
Though you're lying in a puddle—
        Never mind.
If a duckboard barks your shin,
And the barbed wire rips your skin,
'Tis reward for all your sin—
        So never mind.

—:o:—

—:o:—

But this warning I'd attest—
        Have a care.
When your Div. is back at rest—
        Then beware.
When that long three months is over,
And you've lost your canteen cover,
Shoot yourself or find another—
        Have it there !

—:o:—

Have you all your drill forgotten ?—
        Luckless wight.
Through those months so rain besotten—
        Day and night.
On the left you'll form platoon,
Willy nilly, six till noon,
Front line trench will seem a boon—
        Drill's a rite.

—:o:—

Oh ! you poor unhappy thing—
        Be not sad.
Just remember when all's wrong—
        And you're mad.
Though your worries may be great,
They're but part, at any rate,
Of old Fritz's awful fate—
        Buck up, lad !

THE EDITOR much regrets the delay in the production of this number, but the cognocenti will excuse the tardiness on account of disturbed nights, etc.

HOW TO WIN THE WAR.

By BELARY HELLOC.

HAVING very little time at my disposal this week I only intend to roughly outline my plan for ending the war satisfactorily and quickly. Briefly then to do this we must reduce the war to a man to man encounter. Take things like this. The line held on all fronts is 1:500 miles (circa). That is 2,640,000 yards. Now we must get that number of our troops and allot one yard per man. Give each man a bomb, and at a given signal let them all go over and each to account for his own particular opponent. This would account for 2,000,000 of the enemy (that is giving the generous allowance of 640,000 failures), besides putting him to much inconvenience. Each time the enemy brings up reinforcements and re-establishes his line then repeat the performance. I think I may safely say that, after the tenth or eleventh attack, the enemy would be ready to consider the advisability of making terms rather than continue the war. This is merely a rough outline of my plans, and super-ficially it may seem that there are objections. . However, I think these may well be dealt with as they arise.

BELARY HELLOC.

Answers

to Correspondents.

——:o:——

COLONEL.—We are surprised that you should have sent such a story to an earnest periodical like this.

LOVER OF NATURE.—We've had just about enough of you and your birds. The mere fact that you've found a cuckoo's nest with three eggs leaves us cold. If it costs us 500 francs just because you heard a gas-horn and mistook it for the cuckoo, we shudder to think what might happen if we don't nip your natural history nosings in the bud.

SUBALTERN.—Yes, every junior officer may carry a F.M.'s baton in his knapsack, but we think you'll discard that to make room for an extra pair of socks before very long.

KNOWLEDGE.—No, Ypres is not pro-nounced "Wipers" because it was once the centre of the handkerchief industry.

STAFF-OFFICER.—We sympathise with you in your little trouble, and advise you to write to "Cynthia," our love-expert, about it.

ANXIOUS ONE.—No, its no good worrying us. The judge will go through all answers in good time, and the prizes will go to their proper destination. We also regret to say you put ten answers on one coupon, and it's either another nine francs or nothing doing.

"ONE WHO KNOWS"
v.
WIPERS TIMES."

Proceedings in this case were opened at the Courts of Justice, Wipers, on April 20th in the hearing of Mr. Justice Starling. A large crowd was present in court as the case had aroused considerable interest, the Press and naturalists were notably represented.

Counsel for plaintiff—Mr. Cockles Tumley—opened proceedings with a stirring address roundly denouncing the " Wipers Times " for the letter published in their number of March 6th over the nom-de-plume of " A Lover of Nature." This letter he affirmed was untrue and libellous in the extreme, and he thought that this paper exceeded journalistic freedom to an almost criminal extent, and that it ought to be stopped. He finished his address thus :—" The passage chiefly taken exception to reads as follows : ' I am surprised that the editor of a paper with the circulation you boast should have found room for such a scurrilous, lying effusion   The ignorance of the person is visible in every sentence.' This extract undoubtedly throws extreme doubt in the public mind as to the general veracity and knowledge of one of our foremost citizens, and I think I am extremely moderate in asking damages to be assessed at only one million francs.

Mr. Tumley then called various witnesses to prove his client's good standing and social position, and finally the plaintiff himself walked boldly into the box, and took the oath with the utmost assurance and " sang froid."

After putting a few minor questions

Mr Tumley sat down, and Mr. Maurice Aviary—counsel for the defence—rose and hurled a bombshell into the court by asking the plaintiff if he wasn't a leader of one of the bloodthirsty gangs of desperadoes who nightly render Hooge and district " unsafe."

Plaintiff :—It is true that I've been seen in the district in company with other good citizens, though I can't admit of anything but a law-abiding behaviour on my part.

Counsel :—Have you ever entered those well-known dens of vice " The Culvert Dug-out," " Half Way House " or " Railway Wood Dug-out " ?

Plaintiff :—I have, but I disagree with you as to the real nature of these places.

Counsel —Are you a member of the New Night Club adjoining the " Hotel des Ramparts " ?

Plaintiff :—I am, but you are again entirely wrong in your insinuations.

Counsel —Is it not true that you are in great financial difficulties at present ? Now be careful how you answer.

Plaintiff .—I am.

Counsel . —Are you not only bringing this case to see what you can get out of the " Wipers Times " ?

Plaintiff —I am bringing this case to try and clear my good name.

The plaintiff then stood down looking rather less confident of the issue than previously, and Mr Maurice Aviary addressed the jury in his well-known style and love for dramatic effect, concluding with the following words, " I have clearly proved that plaintiff lives by his wits, and consorts with the most doubtful characters, I appeal to you to exonerate my clients, and bring your verdict in accordingly.

After some deliberation, however, the judge eventually said that, although plaintiff was not a man of any great virtues, he thought the paper was wrong in printing the letter, and damages were assessed at 500 francs with costs.

WHAT A HOPE!

The Editor has ordered me
To write a batch of rhymes
To finish off this number of
His bally " New Church Times."

—:o: —

The Editor's a mighty man
His will it must be done,
I'd like to know if he can make
The clock strike less than one
SOME POET.

SPRING-TIME THOUGHTS.

Thank Heaven we are running out of winter and into spring. " Oh, to be in Flanders now that April's there !" Now that summer has begun to arrive naturally everyone is asking " What is going to happen ?" and the air is full of rumours. Is it as impossible for us to go through as it was for the Germans at Verdun ? The differences are distinct contrasts. On the one hand—perfect organisation, but indifferent fighting material. On the other—indifferent organisation, with perfect fighting material. The German is temperamentally a poor uphill fighter, and once his organisation is upset he will crumble. Obviously then the thing is to upset his organisation. The easiest way to do this is to suddenly make him reverse his plan of campaign, and attack him where his organisation is prepared only for attack. The point lying ready to hand for this is obviously Verdun, and, by sudden concentration there, one might achieve an overwhelming success at much less cost than will an organised and obvious push at a place prepared and ready for defence. Neuve Chapelle and Loos show us the cost of breaking through prepared ground, and the result is infinitesimal gain. Possibly the loss would be as large at Verdun, though a well calculated attack there could not easily be more unsuccessful than the two already mentioned. Also it would have the advantages of surprise and of forcing a sudden complete reversal of positions, a state of affairs which might easily prove too difficult for even the German organisation. True, the German artillery is there ready, but so it will be at any front elsewhere. Already the seeds of failure are sown in the German troops there, and it would be easier to turn this into an absolute demoralisation than to butt up against a new army on a new ground.

AMATEUR.

Things We Want to Know.

—:o: —

Who it is that makes an infernal din on a horn at 2 a.m.

? ? ?

Whether it is a fact that the amorous incarnadined major has again succumbed.

? ? ?

EDITORIAL.

AS OUR journal seems to have met with some measure of success, we have pleasure in announcing that the circulation will be increased to 250 copies, commencing with this number. The price will be standard at 1 Fr., which will go towards the purchase of paper, etc., as we are now coming to the end of the supply so kindly left us by some citizen of Wipers who stood not on the order of his going, but got. Any balance over after incidental expenses will go as usual to charity. We regret to say that the district is waning in popularity as a health resort, and several noted citizens have lately been seen " legging it " for pastures new, with a few goods and chattels and some family in tow. We are glad to see that the City Fathers of Wulverghem are going to introduce the Day-light Saving Bill, as this will mean that some soldiers, who are in the district, will be able to go to bed earlier. It really is a great blessing, and will enable all of us who are lovers of nature to take our early morning ramble an hour earlier, thus catching the lark at its best. We are pleased to be able to give the result of our " Last Line " Competition on Page 8. The regrettable efforts made by the competitors have again prostrated the judge, who, I regret to state, is suffering from nervous breakdown as a consequence. Can nothing be done to break the painful monotony of our gas-horns ? Surely they might be fitted with some musical apparatus, and so play say "Excelsior " while arousing the slumbering inmates of Batt. H.Q. Now that summer is coming, we are considering the matter of our Annual Fly Competition. There will be the usual mammoth prizes, but no fly papers will be allowed. Each animal must be fairly shot or bayonetted. Bombing will be allowed, but any gunner found sniping flies with anything larger than an 18-pounder will be disqualified. We will announce in a later issue when the competition will commence, and trust to the honour of all not to start before the flag falls. We hear that the " Douve " mixed bathing season has commenced, and that popular little seaside resort " Le Rossignol " ought to be crowded during the summer months. We must express the hope that we still have the support of the Division in our more ambitious scheme re circulation, and must thank one and all for the appreciation shown to our previous efforts.

THE EDITOR.

If you're waking call me early, call me
    early, sergeant dear.
For I'm very, very weary, and my
    warrant's come, I hear ;
Oh! it's " blightie " for a spell, and all
    my troubles are behind,
And I've seven days before me
(Hope the sea will not be stormy)
Keep the war a'going, sergeant,
Train's at six, just bear in mind !

SIGN POSTS.

There's a line that runs from Nieuport
    down into Alsace Lorraine,
Its twists and turns are many, and each
    means a loss or gain ;
Every yard can tell a story, every foot
    can claim its fee,
There the line will stay for ever from
    Lorraine up to the sea.

Places memorised by symbol, little things
    that caught the mind,
As at Loos 'twas but a lone tree which in
    mem'ry is enshrined ;
Perhaps at Wipers 'twas a corner, shell
    bespattered, held our sight,
Or a nightingale at Plug Street, sending
    music through the night.

Little things, yet each implanted when
    the nerves are tension high,
And in years to come remembered how,
    while gazing, death passed by ;
So the line for all has sign posts, and a
    dug-out oft can hold
Little memories to haunt one as the
    future years unfold.

Though this line will be behind us as we
    push on to the Spree,
Yet to all it will be sacred, mud-encased
    though it may be;
In the future dim and distant they will
    tell the tale again—
The ghosts of those who held the line
    from Nieuport to Lorraine.

QUESTIONS A
PLATOON COMMANDER

SHOULD ASK HIMSELF.

ENGRAVED BY SAPPER COUZENS R.E.

1: Am I as offensive as I might be.

CUPID'S CORNER.
By "CYNTHIA."

AS THE Editor has been so troubled with correspondence from lovelorn members of the Division, and feels that he is not qualified to deal with this section of his readers, he has deputed me to deal with them, and I shall be pleased to give advice in all little difficulties relating to "affaires de cœur."

—0—0—0—

TO MY UNTAMED POET.

Oh, woe is me.   Now, by desire
My head right in the dust I humble ;
Bring sackcloth. ashes, coals of fire,
Pardon I crave that I did stumble.

—§ † §—

My pride has crumbled into naught,
   Like any puff of wind it went,
(I still am half a column short,
   Hence this apology's extent.)

—§ † §—

So pardon that I called thee "tame"
   Who boasts a past so truly blue,
In next week's issue you may claim
The same old page—'tis kept for you.

OUR SPLENDID NEW SERIAL.

—o—o—o—

FROM BUGLER BOY TO BRIGADIER.

OR

How Willie Pritchard Rose from the Ranks

—o—o—o—

A STORY OF THE GREAT WAR.

—o—o—o—

BY RUBY N. DARES.

—o—o—o—

CHAPTER 1.

—o—

WAR! The sleepy old town of Hampton was ringing with the raucous cries of "special-l special!!" for it was a mild summer's evening in the fateful August of 1914. Tradesmen, workmen, artizans were all hurriedly purchasing papers—eagerly scanning the stop press news—the stop press news that sent England reeling under the shattering blow of Germany's perfidy. Groups of men eagerly discussing the news, stood at the street corners of the old town—children ran wildly about, for the moment forgotten by their parents too busily listening to the opinions of their menfolk, and now and then chipping shrilly into the conversation—then came the days of tragic silence—the retreat from Mons, and the urgent appeal for recruits , ...

Such were the early days of the great war in Hampton when Willie Pritchard, the son of honest parents, passed out of the Council School to take his place as salesman in the extensive and well-appointed grocery stores of Sir Jasper Jephcott, the squire of Hampton. When the appeal for King and Country went forth Willie Pritchard's heart was as lead, for had he not an aged mother depending on him for sustenance? How could he go?—how?—ah! that was the question. So Willie stayed on in the grocery store, and hid his aching heart beneath his linen apron. In this manner things went on until one day Sir Jasper suddenly coming from behind a Tate's cube box beheld our hero weeping piteously. "Come, come, William! what is the matter?"—said the kindly old squire, his own voice shaking with emotion—"Are you in any trouble, my lad. Speak! speak!! my little fellow, speak!!!" Dry sobs shook Willie's frame, and for a moment grief poignant and tempestuous held him in her terrible sway, then raising his tear-stained face from his hands he burst forth:—"Sir! Sir!!—I would serve my King!!!"

(What did Sir Jasper say?—See our next instalment.)

Ne'er be peaceful, quiet, or pensive,
" Do your best to be offensive,"
His success shall greatest be,
Who regards this homily.
In the future day and night be
" As offensive as you might be."

WE ARE THE PEOPLE.

YOU WANT IT!! WE'VE GOT IT!!!

THEN COME TO US

DOPE AND CURRIE

Livery and Bait Stables. Registry Offices.

—o—o—o—o—

LESSONS IN DEPORTMENT, Etc., Etc.

—o—o—o—o—

Did I hear you say you wanted a Domestic Servant?

SPLENDID! THEN STEP THIS WAY.

And what for you, Sir—A Charger?

YOU'RE IN LUCK'S WAY---WE'VE THE VERY THING.

—o—o—o—o—

ROLL UP! ROLL UP!! ROLL UP!!!

TELEGRAMS: " VATICAN," BAILLEUL.

EDITORIAL.

SUMMER is really with us at last, and those dreary winter months now only a memory quickly melting in the sun. We are glad to be able to announce that the Division has responded splendidly to our appeal for copy, and in consequence we shall be able to publish much more regularly, provided, of course, that the supply continues. It is gratifying to see the whole hearted support given to this paper, and we should like to take this opportunity of thanking one and all. Also, it is good to see the spirit of cheeriness, unity and understanding which is pervading the whole Division, and which emanates from our G.O.C. and Brigadiers. Our mammoth Competitions are so popular that we must have some more of them as we still have some odd millions to give away. We hope our readers will like the splendid new serial. Each chapter is more enthralling than the last, and when Willie—but there we must keep quiet or we shall be forestalling the author. Our flag day was an enormous success, and our fair staff succeeded in forcing an entrance everywhere. Some of the well-known ladies who assisted are so enthusiastic that they want us to have a flag day regularly. We are considering the idea. Countess Fiveaye made as much as 500 francs for the fund, and the pretty picture presented by the Belle of Berloo getting five francs out of the elegant Staff Captain charmed all beholders. However, the fund for providing " Warm Woollens for War-worn Walloons " has benefited accordingly. We have received several complaints about the " Here to-day and gone to-morrow " methods of a certain firm of Commission Agents who have been advertising in our columns, and our Special Commissioner is investigating same. We must say, however, on our own behalf, that we accepted the advertisement in all good faith, and cannot be held responsible for breach of contract on the part of any of our advertisers. We hear that an eminent firm of financiers is inaugerating a char-a-banc motor service for the summer months, to work in co-operation with the syndicate which has taken over the "Dead Cow" Hotel, so that residents in this delightful district will have the opportunity of moonlight motor trips, pulling up at the famous old hostelry en route. The country is looking particularly well just now, and farmers report things coming up everywhere. As our correspondence has increased to such an alarming extent, we have had to increase our already enormous salary list, and may have to approach the authorities with a view to importing a female staff, and are ready to receive applications for appointments now—publishing side only—as the editorial sanctum must remain quiet. Further Competitions will probably be announced next week. As we have a lot of copy we want to use up, this is our Grand Double Summer Number. The price remains the same as the cover was printed before we struck this brilliant idea. Having originated the idea, however, we intend having a summer number yearly, and the "Empire Day" issue (approx.) will be chosen for the purpose.

THE EDITOR.

AUNT ANNIE'S CORNER.

TENDER TALKS TO TINY TOTS.

—:o:—

My dear little Tot-ties,—

Thank you so much for the nice let-ters you have sent me tell-ing me all a-bout your lit-tle games. Your Auntie al-ways likes to know what her Tots have been doing, and that they have been good chil-dren.

—:o:—

Bertram has wrote to me a long let-ter tell-ing me all a-bout his tin soldiers that a kind friend gave him some time ago. I hope some day some one will give him some more of them.

—:o:—

Roger has a col-lec-tion of pretty pic-tures which he looks at every day. All his lit-tle friends like to look at them too.

—:o:—

Johnnie has a friend named Reggie they go long walks to-geth-er. Isn't that splendid, Tots? Johnnie has a nice lit-tle girl friend that he writes let-ters to some-times.

—:o:—

I want all of you to write to me please, and I will al-ways answer your let-ters if you have been good chil-dren.

Isn't this pretty :—

There was a little man,
He had a little gun,
He shoots it when he can,
But has never hit a Hun.

—:o:—

It was sent to me by a lit-tle friend named Gilbert. He of-ten writes love-ly poet-ry like this. Isn't he clev-er.

Good-bye until next week, Tots.

Your loving,

A DAY FROM THE LIFE OF A "SUB" IN DIVISIONAL RESERVE.

BY HIMSELF.

—o—o—o—

12·40 a.m.—Sleeping peacefully.

12·45 a.m.—Not sleeping peacefully.

12·50 a.m.—Awakened by a noise like a fog-horn gone quite mad.

12.55 a.m.—Realise someone has smelt gas, cannot find gas-helmet or shirt.

1 a.m.—Grope about for matches and candle—find out to my discomfort several extra articles of furniture in the hut—curse volubly.

1·5 a.m.—People rush in to remind me that I am orderly " bloke." Have heated altercation with " next for duty " as to when term of office ends. Matter settled by the entrance of C.O.—AM orderly officer.

1·15 a.m.—Stumble round camp—rumour of " Stand-to "—curse abominably.

1·30 a.m.—Rumour. squashed—gas alarm false — somebody's clockwork motor-bike horn came unstuck—curse again—retire to bed.

3·30 a.m.—Sleeping peacefully.

3·35 a.m.—Alarming noise. Somebody with bigger feet than sense of decency, enters the hut ; and knocks over a bully-beef box doing excellent work as a chair, collides with everybody's field-boots, mistakes my bed for his, and sits down on same— . . . .

3·59 a.m.—Order restored by Company Commander.

6·0 a.m.—Reveillé.

6·30 a.m.—Get up, and wearily put on one or two garments, including somebody else's tie. Spend pleasant moments searching for my wandering collar stud.

7 a.m —Go out and wave my limbs about for 45 minutes to the tune of " Head backward be e-e-nd."

7·45 a.m.—Try to shave—we have one mirror amongst six.

8 a.m.—Breakfast. The cook has plentifully peppered the sausage, put salt in my tea by mistake.

9 a.m.—Take party to and from the baths—one man has no cap badge—collect a bird from Adjutant. Have a bath myself, when nicely soaped the water gives out, becoming mud—curse offensively.

10 a.m.—Orderly room—attend with Company conduct sheets, collect another bird. Make arrangements for a cage and a supply of seed for same.

11 a.m.—Retire to hut and quaff a stoop of ale.

11·5 a.m.—Two in-command arrives inopportunely, speaks his mind and retires.

11·10 a.m.—Inspect my huts and men, their clothes, rifles, gas-helmets, feet, etc.

12 noon.—Realise I am not being as offensive as I might be, so go and annoy the next Company (who were working last night); by creeping in, starting their gramaphone with the loudest, longest and most loathed record, and creeping out again.

12·10 p.m.—Angry " sub " in pyjamas enters. am busy writing letters. After a few choice remarks about people in general and myself in particular, he goes away.

1 p.m.— Lunch.

2 p.m.—Sleeping peacefully.

4·30 p.m.—Tea.

5 p.m.—Fall in working party, astonishing number in my platoon suffer from bad feet at this hour. Discuss their ailment with them, and inspect members affected.

6·30 p.m.—Reach lorries and pack men in. No. 9999 Pte Jones X. falls off and sprains his ankle, and proceeds to camp.

7·30 p.m.—Arrive at rendez-vous and await R.E.

8 p.m.—Await R.E.

9 p.m.—Await R.E.

9·15 p.m.—R.E. arrive in the shape of one most intelligent sapper.

9·30 p.m.—Loaded with material, proceed to job.

9·45 p.m.—My sergeant rushes up. Pte McNoodle, a sheet of corrugated iron, a duckboard, and a crump-hole full of water have got rather mixed. Leave a lance-corporal to straighten matters.

10 p.m.—German machine-gun annoying. Grateful for tin-hat.

1 a.m.—Return to lorries.

2 a.m.—Reach camp and retire to bed.

WAILS TO THE MAIL.
NO. 1.

(Married men of the latest armies will receive 104 pounds per annum in addition to the usual separation allowance.)

Northcliffe, my Northcliffe,
  In days that are dead
The bard was a scoffer
  At much that you said,
A fervid opponent
  Of " Daily Mail " Bread.

The bard never dreamed
  That it mattered a jot
If you trusted in soap
  Or put peas in your pot,
Or how many aeroplanes
  England had not.

And when you backed Blatchford
  To bark at the Bosche,
Or when you puffed Willett
  As wiser than Josh—
Northcliffe, my Northcliffe,
  I own I said " Tosh."

Northcliffe, my Northcliffe,
  Now here at thy feet
The poet craves pardon
  Tho vengeance be sweet
As the peas that thou prizest
  In Carmelite Street.

Forgive me past trespasses,
  Hark to my trope,
To my words that are softer
  Than Lever's Soft Soap,
For only through thee,
  Has a suppliant hope !

Northcliffe, my Northcliffe,
  Ah ! greater than Mars
Or double-faced Janus
  Whose portal unbars
The flood-tide of battle
  Napoleon of " Pars.'

Whose words are uncensored,
  Whose leader compels
Greys, Asquiths, McKennas,
  And eke double L's,
With contraband cotton
  And scandal of shells,

Who rulest the Seas,
  And the Earth and the Air
And the manifold medals
  " Base " Officers wear,
Northcliffe, my Northcliffe,
  Now hark to my prayer !

When the " Hide-the-Truth Press "
  And the " Slack 23 "
Have yielded sword, money,
  And trident to thee
And K.J. and Boosey
  And Pemberton B.

Remember, while paying
  The Derby man's rent,
His rates, his insurance,
  And more than he spent,
That others SAID NOTHING,
  GOT NOTHING, but WENT.

They were somewhere in France,
  While the Derby man bucked
To his wife, and in sheets
  Was connubially tucked . . .
But no one pays them
  For the homes that they chucked.

They were crouching to crumps
  While he cried at a Zepp,
He was dancing what time
  They were taught to "Keep step,"
And he gets a hundred
  Per an. PLUS the Sep-

aration allowance !
  By Carmelite House,
If a Man be worth anything
  More than a Mouse,
Northcliffe, my Northcliffe,
  THESE CHAPS HAVE A GROUSE.

    GILBERT FRANKAU.

22/5/16.

SEMI-DETACHED.

At a lofty elevation
Floating lazy in the sun,
What an ideal occupation
Keeping watch on brother Hun !
—:o:—
Though a " sausage " is my villa
Far from angry whizz-bangs' scream,
I can watch the caterpillar,
And all things are what they seem.
—:o:—
In a contemplative manner
When the " big push " is begun,
'Tis from here I'd love to see it
From my place up in the sun.

THE LECTURE.

If at any time you happen to be
at all depressed—though of course this
is extremely unlikely out here where
there is so much to interest and delight
one—find out whether there is a lecture
on anywhere, given by the G.S.O. first or
second of a Division about to be relieved,
to the officers of the relieving Division,
and go to it at once. It will make you
realise that war is worth while. Roughly
speaking, the show will be as follows :—
The room is packed with an expectant
but nervous conglomeration of officers, of
whom certainly not more than the first
two rows will hear a word of the glad
tidings. That doesn't matter, however
there is a screen and a magic lantern
which you may be deluded into thinking
is going to show you a reasonably clear
picture of the trenches—don't be had by
it—it's only a trap. Well, eventually a
Staff Officer mounts the platform, and
you gather from his opening remarks
that he has been deputed to give the
lecture, that he is not much of a hand at
the job, and that you must forgive him.
This is greeted with sympathetic noises
—the audience apparently attempting to
ingratiate themselves into his good
offices thereby, and hoping that if they
are successful in this he'll let 'em down
with a minimum of forgetfulness. The
Staff Officer is not moved in the least.
He proceeds as follows :—"As a matter of
fact I haven't been up to the front line
for—er—some time (the audience appear
incredible) but when I was last up, A I
had fallen in, and of course most of the
communication trenches had been—er—
crumped in." The audience seem to
appreciate the fact that there are still a
few trenches extant " I will now show
you some photographs of the craters."
The operator having woken up, the
lantern is lit, and a beautiful bright light,
accompanied by a very realistic imitation
of the odours encountered at Hooge is
given. Unfortunately the lighting effects
are poor, but anyway you have a quiet
ten minu'es in which to give your pal
instructions what to do with your corpse.
Eventually a picture is shown, which
may remind you of your late Uncle Bill,
who used to suffer severely from warts.
As the lecturer invariably holds his
pointer at least one foot from the screen,
you will naturally look at the wart
indicated by the shadow, but that always
adds to the amusement, and you can run
a book as to which smudge is the crater.
The grand finale is always worth paying
attention to. " The enemy shoot at you
from three and a half sides, some officers
make it three and three quarters, though
personally I incline to the latter view."
The Staff Officer then tells you that he
doesn't think he has anything more to
say, and though everyone seems grieved
to hear it, he subsides into a chair next
to the G O C. The best part of the
lecture is, of course, that it leaves you
with a magnificent thirst.

P.B.I.

LANCELOT'S LETTERS TO LONELY LADIES.

FLANDERS

May, 1916

YOU poor little Dears :—

How we pity you, how we sob for you, and how often we think of you with great big tender thoughts. I wish we could invite you all to come out here and look round, even in Flanders you would find the country quite charming, in parts, just now, but—on second though s—much as we should love to have you with us, the responsibility of your presence would be too great, but leave being about due we will come home and see you instead.

Tell me, though, do you REALLY all wear those short skirts and things we see such pretty pictures of in the Illustrated Papers from Home?

This is a nice time to come home for a swift, short week is not it? I have visions of little runs to Skindles, lunches at Prince's, " Mr. Manhatten " in the evening and so on, in a land where gas-gongs, whizz-bangs and stand-to's are not allowed.

Are you very much afflicted with " rumourists " at Home? They exist in droves out here, and this is just their busy season. They may be divided into two distinct classes, opti-rumourists and pessi-rumourists. The first named are, at heart, good fellows but save me from the latter. I met one the other night ; said he'd been lunching with some gents of the Corps who " knew things," and that he'd " heard " that the Division was not going out to rest for another five

months, that the Huns were massing in prodigious numbers just opposite our own pet bit of line, and that all leave was on the point of being stopped indefinitely. No, if I've got to mix with rumourists give me the opti type, the sort who has a brother high up in the diplomatic service whom he knows is taking 100 to 8 on the war coming to a satisfactory conclusion by next Thursday week.

I heard such a funny one about one of our majors the other day. He lost his way in a bit of the country he was ill acquainted with. The day was hot and dusty, the major was hot and thirsty when—lo and behold—he saw, leaning in a somewhat negligent attitude against a gate a private soldier.

" Which way to the Officers' Mess of the Umpshires ?" shouted our tired and weary major

" Along the road about half a-mile on the left, sir, answered the Tommy. nodding his head in that direction, but otherwise motionless.

" Why the — — don't you spring to attention when an officer addresses you ? " roared our friend now thoroughly roused

" Because sir " said the man very meekly. " I'm doing F P No 1. and am tied up to this 'ere gate "

And he's a nice little major man too.

Good-bye and God bless you all,

LANCELOT.

Printed &
Published by
Sherwood, Forester &
Co , Ltd.
B.F. F.

THE
KEMMEL TIMES.

WITH WHICH ARE INCORPORATED

The Wipers Times & The "New Church" Times.

No 1. Vol 1.   Monday. 3rd July, 1916.   Price 1 Franc.

EDITORIAL.

MANY startling things have happened since our last number. Firstly there is the death of Lord KITCHENER. True he was known to most of us by name only, yet it was a name that meant a lot to us, and although nothing can make any difference to the result of the war, one would have liked him to have seen that end which he will have done so much to bring about. Then there is the naval victory, which has probably had a great bearing on the duration of the war. Had Fritz been content with saying that, having found more trouble, than he had anticipated, he hit out and ran away, one might have passed it all over, and said that for a Hun he did as well as could be expected. However, the pitiful spectacle of William, Tirpitz and Co. shedding tears of blood in their anxiety to prove to a pack of poor deluded sausage eaters, that they had blown the British Navy off the map, ceases to be amusing and becomes a disgusting spectacle of mono-maniacal absurdity. Meanwhile here everything has been merry and bright. The meat tea and social in aid of the fund for providing blue body belts for bucolic Belgians was an enormous success. Also a very successful sports-meeting was held, which is reported on more fully elsewhere. We are pleased to be able to congratulate many members of the Division on the new and well-earned ribbons which adorn their manly breasts. Also we should like to express the regret felt throughout the whole Division at the temporary disablement of Colonel CUNNINGHAM. and the hopes of all that he will soon be with us again. We have lately heard from several people "in the know " in England that peace is to be declared this month. Should it take place before this issue is before the public, then will all subscribers please call at our offices, when they will be presented with a copy and a gold watch, as a slight remuneration for their kindly support. We are glad to be able to announce another of our mammoth competitions, particulars of which will be found on page 8. The interest which these arouse is very flattering, and we almost feel tempted to increase the prize-money. We must thank the senders of all kindly letters of appreciation of the new serial, and feel that the enormous amount outlaid to secure the rights of this thrilling tale is more than repaid by the satisfaction we have been able to give our readers. It is unfortunate that the weather is so unsettled, as this may detract from the success of the forth-coming regatta on the " Douve." How-ever, we may still hope to see a large and fashionably dressed crowd, as there are many counter-attractions should the weather prove unkind. We must thank those members of the Division who have sent us copy, and express the hope that they will continue, and that many others will also send along something when the spirit moves them. We have lately taken up another and more luxurious suite of offices in a very prosperous neighbour hood, and are consequently compelled once again to change the name of our periodical. We confidently hope to receive the same support from the public as was accorded to the previous journals which are incorporated with the "Kemmel Times."

SPORTS.

On Thursday, the 8th ult., the Royal Fusiliers held a very successful little meeting at Bulford Camp, and Col. Hancock and the officers were at home all the afternoon. The meeting was favoured by very fine weather and was a great success from the word go. There were certain events open to the 24th Division which drew fairly repre-sentative entries, notably the tug-of-war, in which some very interesting heats were decided, to be won finally by an excellent team of the Leinsters who well deserved their victory. Perhaps one of the most interesting events from a spectacular point of view was the Officers V.C. Race which drew about 11 entries, some of the efforts at remounting with the dummy caused a certain amount of good-natured laughter, but the winner showed excellent judgment and skill both in his heat and final. The meeting struck a note that we have more than once advocated in our columns ; a more frequent occurrence of this type of friendly rivalry brings the members of the various units into closer contact with each other, and promotes a greater " Esprit de corps " in the division as a whole, not to mention the relaxation from things more serious which such occasions afford.

As a final word Col. Hancock and his officers were truly excellent hosts, and we thank them one and all for a very enjoyable day, as well as congratulating the executive on the able manner in which everything was carried out.

TO LET.—Fine FREEHOLD ESTATE in salubrious neighbourhood. Terms moderate. Owner going east shortly.—Apply Bosch and Co , Messines.

HOW THE PEASANTS LEFT HOOGE.

VIDE A SPECIAL CORRESPONDENT.

MR. TEECH BOMAS, WRITING ON LAST SCRAP AT HOOGE, IN SEVERAL LEADING LONDON DAILIES.

—.o:—

Of course, as Teech says, it was a thrilling sight to see the peasants of Hooge trekking back to Wipers in the merry month of June. There was Lizzie of the corner estaminet well to the fore, and all the other local celebrities in close attendance. Have you ever seen the peasants of Hooge frolicking in " No Man's Land" and picking gooseberries in Railway Wood ? No ! Well, you surprise me. I really must tell Teech. Bye-the-way, I wonder he did'nt tell us what happened to all the gee-gees in training at the stables. Can't you see those dear peasants calling at the Culvert for a spot before legging it down Menin Road en route to the Hotel des Ramparts where friend Boniface is always on hand to deal out hospitality. That must be SOME glass that Teech uses if, by its aid, he saw the church at Hooge get knocked out of the perpendicular. Poor old church ! What happy hours we can remember in the shadow of its ivy-covered walls (I don't think.) However, on the strength of Teech's observations, the Editor has cut this special reporters salary down to a minimum for missing all these thrilling sights. Well, Tina, it only runs to a bottle of bass to-day, so pour it out clear and I'll tell you all about the British Army.

P.B.I.

Things We Want to Know.

—:0:—

The name of the subaltern who told the Major that to take his wife to Nottingham Goose Fair was like taking a sandwich to the Lord Mayor's Banquet.

? ? ?

Whether the London papers are aware there are a few BRITISH troops on the western front.

? ? ?

What Fritz said when he hurriedly left his sausages the other day.

? ? ?

Whether Tina's knowledge of troop movements is more profitable than her canteen.

Correspondence.

To the Editor,
" Kemmel Times."

Sir,

I feel it my duty to bring to your notice the disgraceful manner in which the Metropolitan Board is carrying out their duties. The countryside is obscured by clouds of dust, and I have yet to see the first water cart operating. Now that the motoring season is in full swing the evil is very apparent, and something should be done at once.

I am, Sir,
Yours Faithfully,
PRO BONO PUBLICO.

—:o:—

To the Editor,
" Kemmel Times."

Sir,

It would appear that a certain amount of uneasiness still prevails among a certain section of your public, as to the bona-fide nature of this Firm. (The enclosed note, value 5 francs, was found shortly after the call of your representative at these Offices, and we have great pleasure in returning same to you.) Doubtless you will see your way to re-assure that section of your public already referred to as to the scrupulous honesty of the firm. The report of your representative which appears in the last issue of your paper, though not unfavourable, does not appear sufficiently definite to remove the feeling of uneasiness in the public mind, which has unfortunately made itself felt lately and caused a considerable decrease in our business.

Yours faithfully,
NUNTHORPE, COX & CO.
June 8th, 1916.

[Our representative asserts that he lost 50 francs. Verb sap.—ED.]

NOTICE.

—:o:—

Owing to pressure on our space, also the many calls on our time by hostile demonstrations in our neighbourhood, we are compelled to hold over numerous answers to correspondents.

HOW TIRPITZ WON THE BATTLE OFF JUTLAND.

Von Tirpitz was an admiral, his beard
 flew bold and free,
He called up all his captains and " My
 gallant lads," quoth he,
" The day has come, ten thousand
 ' Hochs ' and though I stay at home
My spirit will be with you. Now prepare
 to brave the foam ! "

—§ † §—

The captains tried with one accord to
 raise a pleasant grin,
Yet each one wondered when and how
 the trouble would begin ;
Their ships they put in dry dock, had
 the barnacles removed,
While by the aid of countless " steins "
 the outlook they improved.

—§ † §—

" What ho, my merry mariners ! " said
 Tirp. one day in May,
" Art ready now to sweep the sea and
 end Britannia's day ?
Has each of you his Iron Cross, and
 flannel next his skin ? "
With one accord they answered " Ja ! "
 " Gut ! now we can begin ! "

—§ † §—

So Tirpitz crept unto the gate, and peered
 out o'er the sea,
While gravely muttering in his beard
 " I'd rather you than me ! "
" The coast is clear," he shouted back,
 " make haste ' The Day ' is here ! "
Then shut the gate behind them, and
 consoled himself with beer.

—§ † §—

When on his homeward way he paused,
 this master of the gales,
And drove into his statue half a ton of
 six inch nails ;

"Hoch! hoch!" quoth he, "now I
   must go and write up my report
Of this, our greatest victory, and lessons
   it has taught."

—§†§—

So he and Wolff sat down to think, and
   soon one came to see
The mighty German fleet had won a
   glorious victory,
So "wire the news around at once, the
   time is getting short,
The world must have our story ere our
   ships get back to port."

—§†§—

Then back went Tirp. to Kiel again, and
   peeping through the gate
He saw some ships returning in a mighty
   flurried state,
"What's this?" he cried, behind his
   beard his face was turning pale,
And straightway to his statue went and
   drove another nail.

—§†§—

"Ho! ho! my gallant lads," quoth he,
   "why make such frantic haste?
You come as though by devils chased,
   and little time to waste,"
The pale and shaky captains muttered
   through their chattering teeth
"We've won a great big vict'ry, all the
   foe is underneath."

—§†§—

"If that is so" quoth Tirpitz, "why this
   frantic need for haste,
Why not remain and glut on joys of
   which you've had a taste,
Why leave the field of victory whose
   laurels wreath your hair?"
"Well, to be honest 'twas because the
   British fleet was there."

—§†§—

"Oh well!" said Tirp., "the glorious
   news is speeding on its way,
And 'twill be known the whole world 'oer
   ere breaks another day;
If we can't win by ships and guns we
   can at least by tales."
And then into his statue drove another
   ton of nails.

There was a young girl of the Somme,
Who sat on a number five bomb,
  She thought 'twas a dud 'un,
  But it went off sudden—
Her exit she made with aplomb!

People We Take Our Hats off To.

——:o:——

The British Navy.

—:o:—

The Russians.

—:o:—

The French.

—:o:—

The Canadians.

WHO IS IT?

See him standing in his "'plus twos,"
Winking at the girls who pass.;
Note the polish on his brogue shoes,
Always looking in the glass.

See him sitting in his office,
Writing orders for his chief;
See him dashing to his billet,
Keen to see the next releif.

See him writing to the Chateau,
Love has filled his face with glee,
Life no more is dull and flat, oh!
"We will write, love, oft, shall we?"

         STRAFE KAPTING.

Printed &
Published by
Sherwood, Forester &
Co , Ltd.
B.F. F.

THE
SOMME-TIMES.

WITH WHICH ARE INCORPORATED

The Wipers Times, The "New Church" Times & The Kemmel Times:

No 1.: Vol 1.   Monday, 31st July, 1916.   Price 1 Franc.

EDITORIAL.

WELL! Here we are in July with the thermometer still hanging round in the fifties. The war seems to be drawing nearer to its only conclusion, and two or three friends of ours in the Division are thinking of buying a farm at Hooge and settling down immediately they get back from Hunland, although we personally think they would have a much better chance of decent profits if they mined there instead of farmed. The name of the present issue is not yet decided for good and sufficient reasons. By the time these lines appear the 24th Division will be very near its second birthday and, should it be possible at the time, we think it would be a good idea to hold an open ghymkana to celebrate the occasion. On another page is the report of a cricket match held at Locrehof Farm. This was a most interesting event, and the sight of some of our cheery Brigadiers. (the war forgetting, by the war forgot from 2-7 p.m) gambolling on the village green was most inspiring. Our special reporter was there and has done the match in his best style. Also, we have attached to our staff at an enormous salary Mr. Teech Bomas the well-known war correspondent. His thrilling articles will be read with great interest by everyone, especially as he sees incidents overlooked by all others. Our mammoth competition met with the success which has attended its predecessors, and the judge has retired to his dug-out with a case of whisky, 10 sacks of mail and a headache. The result will be published in due course. Our thrilling serial is drawing to its conclusion, and we are making arrangements for another Herlock Shomes story. We also hope to introduce several new features shortly, including another mammoth competition. Should this issue be very much delayed we hope our readers will understand and excuse it on account of the many calls on our time. Since the above was written certain things have happened which have decided the name of the present issue. Whether we shall have time or not to fill all the pages is another thing, and our readers will understand if the number is produced with a blank page or two. We think it better to take this course than wait till after the show to produce a full number. And now there is one thing we would wish to do, that is, to wish God-speed to all our pals in the Division. We've all had many weary and many good times together. Who that has known it can forget the joy of a spot in the Culvert dug-out, and the many other haunts known to most of us? Whatever comes we can rely on the old Division to give a good account of itself. So here's to you all, lads, the game is started, keep the ball rolling and remember that the only good Hun is a dead Hun. Good luck be with you all, and when we pull out—well—call in at the editorial sanctum for a spot and a chin.

THE EDITOR.

TO MINNIE.

(Dedicated to the P.B.I.)

In days gone by some aeons ago
That name my youthful pulses stirred,
I thrilled whene'er she whispered low
Ran to her when her voice I heard.

—:o:—

Ah Minnie! how our feelings change,
For now I hear your voice with dread,
And hasten to get out of range
Ere you me on the landscape spread.

—:o:—

Your lightest whisper makes me thrill,
Your presence makes me hide my head,
Your voice can make me hasten still—
But 'tis away from you instead.

—:o:—

You fickle jade! you traitrous minx!
We once exchanged love's old sweet tales
Now where effulgent star-shell winks
Your raucous screech my ear assails:

—:o:—

No place is sacred, I declare,
Your manners most immodest are,
You force your blatant presence where
Maidens should be particular.

—:o:—

You uninvited do intrude,
You force an entrance to my couch,
Though if I've warning you're about
I'll not be there, for that I'll vouch.

—:o:—

Name once most loved of all your sex,
Now hated with a loathing great,
When next my harassed soul you vex
You'll get some back at any rate,

GOD-SPEED.

For a year we've taken what came along,
We've fought or worked and we've held
our line,
Till August finds us " going strong,"
The game's afoot and the goal's the
Rhine.

—:o:—

Through summer's heat and the winter's
gloom
We've tasted the joys that the Salient
holds,
A filthy dug-out our only room,
Where our only comfort a jar enfolds.

—:o:—

We've learnt the game in a grim hard
school,
Where mistakes had a price that 'twas
hard to pay,
With Death sitting by and holding the
rule,
And conducting our studies by night and
day.

—:o:—

But we've also learnt, and 'tis good to
know,
That the pal of a dug-out's a friend worth
while,
For friendship made 'neath the star-shell's
glow
Means " Help every lame dog over a
stile."

—:o: -

Now we have arrived in pastures new,
Where the Hun's taking lessons that
once he gave.
Here's the best of good luck to all of you
In the teaching of blackguards how to
behave.

CRICKET.

—o—

WITH APOLOGIES TO CAPT. F. B
WILSON (Late of the Daily Mirror.)

—o—

X. I. B. v. LOCREHOF.

—o—

It was a great game, we won of course,
and Roger Rum got a blob, bless him.
Anyway I won ten bob, and how Johnny
did love it. Small wonder too, as he
had actually registered more'n forty on
the tins before he had his middle ash
rather badly bent, watching 'em like the
meanest private watches dear Minnie at
Spanbroekmolen and connecting every
time too he was. What an innings, in
other words the real bons. As for the
Editor he revelled in it—he is rather
roguish with the crimson rambler. Was
I there? Search me as they say in Horace,
AND I may tell you that the day before
when the Editor was batting I removed
all three pegs with the second ball (the
only reason it was'nt the first was because
I'd previously arranged to let him get a
couple by serving up a full toss well
outside the crux peg providing he did the
same to me when I staggered into the
centre) well, as I've said, the Editor got
a couple and then went out—quick—and
during the remainder of the innings proceeded to prop up the bar at the regimental canteen during closed hours too—
the horrid florid Forester ! By the time,
therefore, I took my stand he'd forgotten
all about our little do, and hanged if the
very first time he swung the spheroid at
me it was'nt accompanied by a fearful
crash of ash. He's no sportsman as you
may or may not know, but I'm getting
a trifle off the rails so I'll continue. The
Professor turned up for a moment, and
we assured him we weren't playing too
much cricket but merely combining same
with a little bombing practice. And
what about our sometime Rugger international ? I don't care to tell you how
many he got as he's my C.O. so ask the
Editor if you want the news. The
wicket was as beautiful as Tina, and we
had a priceless day although Bobbie
was'nt playing.

P.B.I.

A MESSAGE FROM MR. TEECH BOMAS.

BY OUR SPECIAL CORRFSPONDENT MR TEECH BOMAS.

—:o:—

MR TEECH BOMAS SPEAKS.

—:o:—

No Man's Lard, 20/7/16.

I write from the middle of the battlefield. There are a lot of bullets but I don't mind that. Also the air is thick with shells. That also I don't mind. Let me tell you all about it while I can think clearly. Before the battle commenced I took up a favourable position in No Man's Land, the little larks were larking and the morning was fine. Ther Hell broke loose and as things got really hot I climbed up the rope of a sausage and joined two A.S.C.'s who were also watching the proceedings. Let me tell you of the gallant dash of the Umpshires: Into the pick of the Prussian Guard they dashed. The few of the Guard who remained cried "Kamerad" and surrended. That rush was epic. I then walked over the German lines to have a look at them. There were a lot more bullets but what would you? Now I thrill with an ecstacy. Here they come, the wood is ours. Strange associations, here we see the submarine co-operating with the cavalry and shells falling thickly. Then—the peasants—I witnessed the thrilling scenes of the last peasants leaving their happy farms in No Man's Land, harnessing their mongrel dogs into their little carts and driving off when the battle got a bit hot. It was epic. Taking a place is one thing but putting it back is another. Profound but true, and so the wood was won. A correspondent must always see to write. This may appear unnecessary to the cognoscenti, but it is so. To-morrow I will tell you more. I return now to the battle.

H. TEECH BOMAS.

TRENCH CONVERSATIONS.

—o—o—o—

NO I.

—:o:—

KIND COMPANY COMMANDER (To Man in Trench)—"That aeroplane's a bit low?" MAN IN TRENCH—"Yes, sir." K.C.C.—"It's a Boche, isn't it?" M.I.T.—"Yes, sir." K.C.C.—"I don't seem to know your face, are you one of the latest drafts?" M.I.T.—"No sir, I'm a gunner." K.C.C.(musing)—"That's the worst of these Batt. Lewis Gunners, one never gets to know them." (Aloud) "I suppose you often fire at Boche aeroplanes when they fly low?" M.I.T.—"No, sir." K.C.C.—"Haven't you got any A.A. mountings for your gun?" M.I.T.—"No, sir." K.C.C.—"Well, of course, even if you haven't its really quite simple for you to fire your gun from the shoulder, isn't it? M.I.T.—"No sir, it 'ud be 'ard to get the right amount of elevation, it would." K.C.C.—"Why, my man?" M.I.T.—"'Cos I'm the signalling corporal for the 4·5 Howitzer Battery coverin' yer, and it 'ud give yer a bit of an 'eadache firing the ruddy gun from the shoulder, it would!"—(COLLAPSE OF K.C.C.)—The war proceeds. [P.B.I.

ALBERT - POZIERES - BAPAUME CIRCUIT.

—o—o—o—o—

Grand Touring Concert Party,

BY SPECIAL ARRANGEMENT WITH

PROFESSOR SCRAPPER.

—o—o—o—o—

THE FOLLOWING WILL BE THE PROGRAMME (W.P.)

—o—o—o—o—

TROUPE OPENING CHORUS.

1. Song—"When the midnight choo-choo leaves for Pozieres."

2. Solo—"Up I came with my little lot."
   Enrico WALTHALLO.

3. Concerted item—"Come along over the garden wall."
   BY THE TROUPE.

4. Grand chorus and glee—"I'm much more happy than when I was free."
   Sung by Messrs. BOSCH.

5 Song and Chorus—"Pray tell me gentle Hunlet are there any more at home like you."

6 Grand concerted number—"Another little drink would'nt do us any harm."
   BY THE TROUPE.

—o—o—o—o—

BOOK EARLY. PRICES DOUBLE.

77

OUR MAMMOTH COMPETITION.

We have great pleasure in announcing that the 1st and 2nd prizes of the above Competition have again been won by the Editor and Sub Editor respectively with the following praiseworthy efforts. We reprint the verse in toto for the edification of those who were not fortunate enough to see it.

There was a fair Belgian of Loere,
Who smothered herself with red ochre,
    When people asked why
    She exclaimed with a sigh,
The following line was successful in gaining the 1st prize :—

I'M SUCH AN INVETERATE JOKER.

The 2nd prize was awarded for the following line :

I'VE FALLEN IN LOVE WITH A
                    STOKER

As usual no other efforts were worthy of consideration, so we were compelled to return the balance of the prize money to our bank.

Correspondence.

To the Editor,
    "Somme-Times."

Sir,

I should like to draw your attention to a recent discovery of ours which we have made by judicious inter-breeding. It is the "Parrotidgin" and it is the result of crossing the parrot and the pigeon. It should be of immense use to the War Office as the bird can deliver its message by word of mouth. It requires careful feeding and judicious handling. Our efforts in this direction are still proceeding and we will advise you of any further results.

We are, sir
    Yours faithfully,
        GRANDPA and NICKETT,
            Ornithologists.

Things We Want to Know.

—o—

The name of our most recent encarnadine acquisition who has a pretty taste in visiting cards and where he got them.

? ? ?

The name of the brunette infantry officer who succumbed to measles of the Hun variety and where he caught them.

? ? ?

Whether most of the Division goes to the BIG Town to see the CATHEDRAL.

? ? ?

Whether we still have the Munque collection of Old Masters with us and if there have been any recent additions.

On account of the many calls on our time and space we are compelled this week to curtail the space allotted to our Correspondence and Answers to Correspondents.

TRENCH CONVERSATIONS.

—o—o—o—
NO II.
—:o:—

SUB.(To man wearing cardigan over shirt on blazing hot day)—' What the deuce are you wearing your cardigan for on a day like this ? "

MAN.—To keep my shirt clean, sir !

The Kaiser once said at Peronne
That the Army we'd got was " no bon,"
    But between you and me
    He didn't " compris "
The size of the job he had on

THE
B. E. F. TIMES.

WITH WHICH ARE INCORPORATED

The Wipers Times, The "New Church" Times, The Kemmel Times & The Somme-Times.

No 1. Vol 1.   Friday, 1st December, 1916.   Price 1 Franc.

EDITORIAL.

 A LONG time has elapsed since our last number. This was unavoidable, in fact at one time it seemed that our tenth number would also be our last, as the press was marooned in the midst of a disturbance which is taking place down South. However the outfit is once more safely housed, and our new premises, although draughty, are at least in a quieter situation where the street calls and other noises are not so persistent. Many cheery faces are missing from the Division; and it seems we must get a new lot of contributors. For reasons over which we have no control we are compelled to alter the title of our journal, and so we now appear under the all-embracing name of "The B. E. F. Times." May we here and now beg everybody to send along every incident which might be adapted, humorous or otherwise. We have great pleasure in announcing that, for an enormous fee, we have secured another effort from the pen of the author of "Herlock Shomes." Owing to the popular demand some characters of the story have been resuscitated, we will leave to the reader's imagination how they got over the little difficulties in which the end of the last serial saw them. The first instalment appears in this number. We are fortunate in having another graphic article from our special correspondent Mr. TEECH BOMAS. Also we have opened a new branch in "Our Matrimonial Column," and any candidates for a suitable partner can probably be accommodated from the splendid selection of charming young ladies we have on our books. For this branch we have secured the services of "the brunette

81

infantry officer" whose graceful figure and bronzed complexion were such a feature at Prince's and the Piccadilly Grill Room in the dear dead days when we fondly imagined war to be other than wallowing in a dirty ditch. It was all very well for NAPOLEON to shout about every soldier carrying a Field Marshal's baton in his knapsack, after all he knew very little of war. The nearest approach nowadays is a tin of bully in a sandbag, and anyway even if you had a "Field Marshal's baton," then you'd have to dump it to make room for another pair of socks or you'd be over 35 lbs. We have an article from our special correspondent, who has just spent two years in a German front line trench disguised as a Hun. He had breakfast with the Crown Prince, and relates his experiences in a thrilling article. We have pleasure also in announcing a new competition. We should like to extend a welcome to all those who have recently joined the Division, and to express the hope that they will try to assist us by sending along copy. This also applies to all other units of the B. E. F., and we hope to receive enough copy to enlarge our numbers to 12 pages.

THE EDITOR.

TOMMY IN FRANCE.

—0—0—0—

"Oh! madamerselle, chery madamerselle,
　　You come for a nice promenay?
Yes, its always the same with your ' apres
　　la guerre,'
And your ' me no compris ' what I say,
Come along Bill to the old ' staminet,'
Though the beer may be rotten it still is
　　a ' wet,'

A hunk off a loaf and a glass, me and you,
What's that old lady? Oh! damn it,
　　' Napoo.' "

—:o:—

Q.

" O.C. Companies will render a return,"
'Tis imperative that Q. should quickly
　　learn,
　　If you're short a tin of bully
　　Please investigate it fully,
" O.C. Companies will render a return."

—:o:—

By the 16th inst. the O.C. Coys will state
If they've got an engine driver or a mate,
　　Or if some benighted private
　　Ever managed to arrive at
Excellence in sticking coal into a grate.

—:o:—

Are your men nonconformistic'ly inclined,
When you've had your cheese what
　　happens to the rind?
　　Why was plum and apple jam
　　Substituted for the ham?
And your " eskimo " return is much
　　behind.

—:o:—

Is your Company addicted to trench
　　feet?
Do you save the bones from out your
　　daily meat?
　　Have you men who can hew lumber
　　If so kindly send the number,
Is your S.A.A. affected by the heat?

—:o:—

Do you wonder at the awful careworn
　　smile
On the face of every O.C. Coy, the
　　while
　　In his sleep you'll hear him murmur
　　" Have I got a man from Burma,
Or a sergeant who can go and dam the
　　Nile? "

FRAGMENTS FROM FRANCE.

—:0:—

And it came to pass in the early forenoon, having partaken of a frugal meal of clorinated tea and Tickler, I sallied forth and gained the chalky fastnesses of WHISKY CRATER, completely oblivious of the dangers I encountered from our own artillery and Tock Emmas! Scorning the periscope, I slowly elevated my bust above the parapet.

" Jee-rusalem—surely this is not the result of excessive thorassic lubrication? No, no, a thousand times NO! It cannot be since last night the Quartermaster once more failed us, and the Army Service Corps had registered another hit."

There, before my startled gaze appeared the familiar form of Ginger Fritz of Doodles!

Alas! What memories that name conjures up! Fritz of Doodles!

But, what a change!

Quantum mutatus ab illo as we used to say in our schooldays!

Gone was the greasy evening dress, and in its place the field grey uniform.

Gone too his happy smile, and in its place a look of concentrated hate.

He stopped! He looked! He listened! Then he saw me.

With true Prussian instinct he levelled his musket and pointed it in my direction.

Like a flash an inspiration seized me! "Waiter" I cried at the top of my voice. " Waiter! A brandy and soda! A bun for the lady friend!"

At the sound of the well-known voice he started; his lethal weapon clattered to the ground, and with leaps and bounds he answered the call.

In two of the proverbial shakes he was beside me in the trench.

As I led my now smiling prisoner down the C.T. I had visions of how I would spend my week's leave. Doodles of course would be one of my first calls!

I was about to thank Fritz for the good turn he had done me, when I suddenly thought of A.O. 1965/3 . . . damm it all! I forget the rest of it—but I do remember that I can't go on leave for at least another four months,

VIRTUE.

Now you subs of tender years
For your morals, it appears,
(You must admit they're open much to
question)
There is shortly going to be
A morality O.C.,
Who will see that vice does not spoil
your digestion.

His H.Q. is going to be
Close by Leicester Square, and he
Will parade his Batt. for duty everynight,
In his ranks we'll shortly see
P'raps a Bishop or M.P.,
Who will see that virtue's path you tread
aright.

If on leave and pleasure bent
At Victoria, a gent
Will grab you as you're dodging off alone,
Will escort you to H.Q.,
When you'll quickly find that you
Are provided with an aged chaperone.

Your amusement will depend
On how much she'll let you spend,
And you'll dine at Lyons or an A.B.C.,
Should you dare to want a drink,
With a look she'll make you think
What an awful well of sin a sub can be.

You may smoke one cigarette,
Ere retiring you will get
All your orders for the morrow's pleasure
feast,
Hand your cash in charge, and then
Off to bed as clock strikes ten,
Feeling that in former days you were a
beast.

You will come to learn and love
Programmes as described above
For you must admit that you were most
immoral,
You will find when leave's expired
That your fancies will have tired
For the glass that sparkles, and for lips of
coral.

MY IMPRESSIONS.

—:o:—

BY THE MAN WHO HAD BREAK-FAST WITH THE CROWN PRINCE.

—:o:—

AFTER a lot of manœuvring, I had managed to obtain an interview with the Staff Officer who was in charge of the Prince's valuable collection of "Objets de vertu." As I was perfectly disguised as a Bond Street Art Dealer my task was made much easier. By way of opening up the conversation I commented on a beautiful painting which I was told the Prince had bought from a poor Belgian woman After several hours conversation, during which I extolled the virtues of all the Prince's purchases, I was invited to take breakfast with the Prince himself What a heavensent opportunity. Of course I accepted with alacrity, and was shortly ushered into his own apartments " Hullo " said the Prince with his usual jocularity " How's your father " " My parent is enjoying his usual health I thank your Highness " I replied "May I venture to ask, how you are progressing at Verdun?"

" Verdun be damned " howled this spoilt favourite of fortune. "I never want to hear of the place again I was there, or at least near there some days ago, and made a speech to my soldiers — jolly good speech it was too—all the fancy bits about father and myself and ' places in the sun,' and that even if they were all, killed I'd remember 'em in my prayers before turning in and the damned ungrateful fellows didn't even give me a ' hoch.' Father was cross " !

" And may I ask your Highness " I ventured, " How is his Imperial Majesty, your father." " Rotten " candidly replied the Prince, " He's really fed up with old Tirpy and Falky. You see, Tirpy told him either to go away, or come and run the damned fleet himself, and when papa told Tirpy that, as far as he could see, the fleet ran itself, Tirpy got cross and shot a poor old woman who was just going to knock a nail in his statue. So between the lot of them, life is becoming unbearable. Papa is so hasty."

" And may I ask your Highness's opinion of the military situation ? " I ventured.

" Tophole " the Prince replied with enthusiasm. " If it lasts five or six years longer I shall have one of the best collections in the world."

" And the new English Army " I slyly remarked.

" Pah " snapped the Prince, as he savagely spat at his orderly " You wait till I've finished with Verdun, I'll attend to them."

Seeing that the interview was over, I took my leave and went, feeling confident that my disguise was unpenetrated.

Stop Press News.

—:o:—

GREAT ROBBERY AT THE MUNQUE ART GALLERIES.

—'o·—

We regret to announce that a burglary has taken place at the Munque Art Galleries. This valuable collection of old masters has been stolen and evidence points to an old hand at the game. Suspicion has fastened on William, jun., the Potsdam pincher. No further details yet to hand.

Generals von Sauerkraut and Hauptmann von Götzer wish to pair for the winter. Any acceptances should be addressed to O.C. Huns. Bapaume.

We hear that a traverse has been sunk at P 42 C 1·3. It is feared that this is likely to be a total loss. Submarines are suspected.

Miss Minnie Werfer arrived at the front, but went off suddenly.

TO THE P.B.I.

AN APPRECIATION.

Gone is the Summer, and gone are the
flies,
Gone the green hedges that gladdened
our eyes ;
Around us the landscape is reeking
with rain,
Gone is all comfort—'tis Winter again.

—§ † §—

So here's to the lads of the P.B.I.,
Who live in a ditch that never is dry ;
Who grin through discomfort and danger
alike,
Go " over the top " when a chance comes
to strike ;
Though they're living in Hell they are
cheery and gay,
And draw as their stipend just one bob
per day.

—§ † §—

Back once more to the boots, gum, thigh,
In a pulverised trench where the mud's
knee-high ;
To the duck-board slide on a cold wet
night,
When you pray for a star-shell to give
you light ;
When your clothes are wet, and the rum
jar's dry,
Then you want all your cheeriness, P.B.I.

—§ † §—

They take what may come with a grouse
just skin-deep,
In a rat-worried dug-out on mud try to
sleep ;

Do you wonder they make all the
atmosphere hum,
When some arm-chair old lunatic grudges
them rum ;
And they read in the papers that "James
So-and-Such
Thinks that our soldiers are drinking too
much."
Leave the Tommy alone Mr. James
So-and-Such.
There are vices much nearer home waiting
your touch ;
Take yourself now for instance, examine
and see
If your own priggish virtue is all it
should be ;
Give those of a larger life chance to enjoy
A charity wider than that you employ.

—§ † §—

Don't let Tommy's vices shatter your
sleep,
When you write to the " Times " stick
to " Little Bo-Peep,"
As a subject she's really much more in
your line
Than licentious soldiery, women, and
wine,
So here's to the lads who can live and
can die,
Backbone of the Empire, the old P.B.I.

PIONEER.

Who Invented The Tanks ?

—o—o—o—

We notice much discussion going on in our English contemporaries re the inventorship of the tanks. We could settle the matter here and now, but modesty compels us to keep the matter secret. If they have been helpful in winning the war we are content.

The prisoner with mournful look just
    sadly murmured " Who'd
Have thought that Prussia's best should
    thus so quickly have been looed ?"
" Ho yus," said Tommy with a grin, "and
    bloomin' well napooed."

HOW THE TANKS WENT OVER.

—:o:—

BY OUR SPECIAL CORRESPONDENT,
Mr. TEECH BOMAS.

—:o:—

In the grey and purple light of a September morn they went over. Like great prehistoric monsters they leapt and skipped with joy when the signal came. It was my great good fortune to be a passenger on one of them How can I clearly relate what happened ? All is one chaotic mingling of joy and noise No fear ! How could one fear anything in the belly of a perambulating peripatetic progolodymythorus. Wonderful, epic, on we went, whilst twice a minute the 17in. gun on the roof barked out its message of defiance. At last we were fairly in amongst the Huns. They were round us in millions and in millions they died. Every wag of our creatures tail threw a bomb with deadly precision, and the mad, muddled, murderers melted. How describe the joy with which our men joined the procession until at last we had a train ten miles long. Our creature then became in festive mood and, jumping two villages, came to rest in a crump-hole. After surveying the surrounding country from there we started rounding up the prisoners. Then with a wag of our tail (which accounted for 20 Huns) and some flaps with our fins on we went. With a triumphant snort we went through Bapaume pushing over the church in a playful moment and then steering a course for home, feeling that our perspiring panting proglodomyte had thoroughly enjoyed its run over the disgruntled, discomfited, disembowelled earth. And so to rest in its lair ready for the morrow and what that morrow might hold. I must get back to the battle   TEECH BOMAS.

OUR MATRIMONIAL COLUMN.

—:o:—

Everything in this department receives the greatest discretion and secrecy, and correspondents may be assured that all correspondence is treated with the utmost delicacy.

—:o:—

CAPTAIN.—35, handsome and dashing appearance. Thoroughly domesticated and capable of looking after the home. Feels lost in his present position of Camp Commandant. Fond of dogs. Would welcome correspondence with a view to matrimony. Money no object as he has his pay.—Write Vatican, c/o this paper.

—.o:—

BRIG GENERAL.—Young — charming personality—feels lonely Bashfulness has made him take this way of settling his future happiness, and he would like to correspond with some priceless· young lady matrimonially inclined.—Write Rudolph, c/o this paper.

— :o:—

—:o:—

BRIG.-GENERAL. — Companiable—jocose—domesticated—loving. Is feeling his unattached condition very much, and seizes this opportunity of making overtures to some sympathetic young lady. — Write Jock, c/o this paper.

—:o:—

LIEUT.-COLONEL. — Gone grey through loneliness. Feels that his life could be brightened by the introduction of a female element. Romantic disposition, and has had many " affaires," but would entertain an opportunity of settling down Widow preferred. Money no object, but would like one with small public house—Write Buffs, c/o this paper.

—:o:—

LIEUT.-COLONEL.—Tall and striking appearance. Just recovered from wound, feels lost now without feminine attentions, and would welcome correspondence that might ultimately end in providing him with congenial society for life.—Write Rugger, c/o this paper.

—:o:—

(Many thousand advertisements are held over for lack of space.)

THE WAR LORD AND THE CHANCELLOR.

(With apologies to the late Lewis Carrol..)

The War Lord and the Chancellor,
  Were walking hand in hand ;
They laughed like anything to see
  The devastated land ;
" If this belonged to us," they said,
  " It really would be grand."

—0—0—0—

" If fifty Huns with fifty guns,
  Swept it for half a year ;
Do you suppose," the War Lord said,
  " That vict'ry would be near ? "
" I doubt it," said the Chancellor,
  And shed a bitter tear.

—0—0—0—

" You always were a pessimist,"
  The frowning War Lord said ;
" Oh ! Highest One it is because
  I always look ahead ;
Before this War is finished you
  And I will both be dead."

—0—0—0—

" Don't talk like that I do beseech,"
  The War Lord wailed aloud ;
" To win this War by any means,
  You know that I have vowed ;
With Zeppelins and submarines,
  And waves of poison cloud."

—0—0—0—

" Oh ! chuck it Bill," the Chancellor
  Said with a rueful air,
" You know quite well with 'frightfulness'
  We've tried them everywhere.
And got it back with interest,"
  Bill glared and tore his hair.

—0—0—0—

He danced with rage, he howled and
    swore,
  And vowed that he would see
That Army so contemptible
  Would very quickly be
By every kind of " frightfulness "
  Sent to eternity.

—0—0—0—

The Chancellor spoke loud and long,
  With rhetoric inspired ;
He spoke of love. and peace, and food,
  He spoke till he was tired ;
And when he paused he turned around—
  The War Lord had expired !

Extracts From Contemporaries.

—0—0—0—

1.—(From " Corps Intelligence Summary," Nov. 1/14.)—" ALARMS.—Dogs have been HEARD BARKING in the trenches and ALSO GEESE. Confirmation is required as to whether the geese are in the trenches or wild geese flighting."

2.—(From " John Bull," Nov. 18/16.)—" The case of a certain BATTALION of the Duke of Wellington's Regiment is instanced to us. FIFTEEN THOUSAND STRONG, they 'have been at Skipton, Derby, etc. . . "

SHATTERED ILLUSIONS.

—o—o—o—

It may be love that makes the world go
round,
Yet with the statement oft I disagree ;
It was not love (on that I'll bet a pound)
That, last night, made the world revolve
round me.

—o—o—o—

I cannot bring my mind to realise
That love inspired friend Fritz, when he
propelled
A Minnie of a most terrific size
In my direction, so, I had him shelled.

Peace, peace, let us have peace,
Quoth Bill with a face grave and long ;
You can see we have won
Ere you've really begun,
So let's chuck it while I'm going strong.

THE WAR IN THE EAST.

—:o:—

Major Taude, B.C.

—:o:—

Of course all the tactics employed in
this campaign are wrong. I have studied
the whole affair carefully (from maps and
the histories of previous wars) and I find
them absolutely contrary to all the rules
laid down by Julius Caesar and Hannibal.
I well remember the excellent results
obtained by my adoption of the tactics
used by Bruce at Bannockburn, and I
consider that it was due to these that I
obtained the splendid moral victory over
the Church Lads' Brigade, at Shepherd's
Bush, in 1870. I have proved time and
again in my articles that the opposing
force can only hope for success so long
as it beats the defending force, and that,
once the positions are reversed, then the
defending force will become the attacking
force. War and tactics have been my
constant study, and I feel sure that a
more careful scrutiny of my works would
lead to an earlier successful termination
of the war. There was that successful
little affair of mine at Clapham Common
which might be emulated with advantage
by Sir Douglas Haig in his Western
campaign. Verb. sap.

OUR SHORT STORY.

—:o:—

It was Xmas morning in the trenches !
M-m-m-m-m.

Printed &
Published by
Sherwood, Forester &
Co., Ltd.
B.E.F.

PALACE OF VARIETIES, L---- (CENSORED ED)

—o—o—o—o—

POSITIVELY THE GREATEST COLLECTION OF ENTERTAINERS WHICH HAS EVER BEEN GOT TOGETHER AT ONE PLACE AND TIME.

FOR ONE WEEK ONLY.

—o—o—o—o—

Miss MINNIE WERFER.

ALWAYS MEETS WITH A THUNDEROUS RECEPTION.

—o—o—o—o—

THE ALLIMAN FAMILY—Glee Singers.

COMPLETELY NEW NUMBERS, INCLUDING :—

"La Paloma," "They Didn't Believe Me."

—o—o—o—o—

The Irish Troupe Of Quick Change Artists.

IN THEIR AMUSING SKETCH,

"Won't You Come and Play in Our Yard."

—o—o—o—o—

GRAND OPERETTE, ENTITLED :—

WILLIAM, TELL!

GRAND MALE CHORUS.

AS PERFORMED BEFORE MOST OF THE CROWNED HEADS OF EUROPE. DURING WHICH BETHMANIANO WILL SING

"I Would Row Wilson if Wilson Would Row Me."

—o—o—o—o—

PRICES DOUBLE. BOOK EARLY.

ANTI-ZEPPELIN CURTAIN LOWERED TWICE NIGHTLY.

EDITORIAL.

NOW we have arrived at our "Grand Double Xmas Number" (this by-the way is provided the paper arrives in time) and the first thing any good Editor does, is to wish all his readers the very best of good wishes. Between ourselves I think the least said about "Peace on earth, goodwill to man" the better, when most of the inhabitants of this planet are trying to "put it across" someone or other in the most unpleasant way that lies handy. We have received many of the Xmas Nos. of our English contemporaries, and we must say that it is about time England had a war, if the popular taste runs in the direction indicated by most of the coloured plates. It is good to see that England has at last realised that we are at war, and has fixed the price of officers meals, although we fully endorse the views expressed by the Brigadier who wanted an extra pat of butter at an A.B.C. and was told he had already spent ninepence, and so was up to his limit. But it is undoubtedly a step in the right direction, and by the time the war is in full swing it will not surprise us to see many innovations of this sort, in fact, one might venture to prophecy that a few more years of war, will see officers restricted to a three shilling taxi fare. If we are to win the war then officers will really have to make every sacrifice. But it is pleasing to see that England has shaken herself and means business. Also we think that our contemporary the "Daily Mail" should be suppressed. It is always urging some drastic step, and calling attention to the war. In fact, so strong and persistent at times became its hysterical shouting, that some decisions were actually reached. All this is very unnerving, and we really think that the total suppression of the Northcliffe Press is the only way of ensuring the preservation of a respectable and dignified " festina lente " policy. Should the war be hurried we, the Editor, would lose our job, and so would many others, a fate horrible to contemplate. Out of work, and thrown on the mercy of a hard and cruel world, good heavens ! Put more coal on the fire ! My dug-out has suddenly become chilled. A bas Northcliffe a bas " Daily Mail ". Taisez vous ! Mefiez vous ! Les oreilles ennemies vous ecoutent ! During our nocturnal rambles the other night, when the country was bathed in a soft light, the joint production of moon and star shell, we met a PESSIMIST. He was a strange elfish creature, and seemed in the depths of despair. A broken rum jar at his side, and the mute evidence of his appearance testified to the utter abandonment of all hope. He opened up the conversation with the remark " We've lost this 'ere war." " Come cheer up old chap all is not yet over" we remarked in a futile endeavour to throw a little light into the darkness " Hover " he exclaimed as he took off a gum boot and emptied a stream of liquid mud into a dixie full of tea belonging to the next dug-out. " Ho, then yer don't read the papers. 'Ere's Ilarious Belloc says all's lost in the East, 'ere's Bottomley says we're sitting on a volcano, and a lump of pineapple gone t'hrough the rum jar. I'm going over the top to kill a 'un. I'm that fed up."

Seeing the impossibility of disputing his point we passed on, deep in thought. " Surely, surely," we thought " they must realise everything possible is being done. Here we have officers meals limited to five shillings, and they're not to wear evening clothes any longer. Good heavens ! Can the fellow not realise what an effort we are making. And so we returned home, saddened by our experience, and killed three rats on the way in the irritation of the moment. But this, by-the-way, is our Xmas Number and we have rather side-tracked :

" Good King Wenceslas looked out
On a frosty morning."

Can you imagine a picture of " Good King Wenceslas" sticking his nose out of a dug out and saying what he thought of war in general, and Huns in particular? Try and imagine the dear old lad as a platoon commander at " stand to " on a Xmas morning ! He'd have carolled some We have great pleasure in announcing that our new Mammoth Competition will be found on the last page. We are awaiting news of several new and interesting features which we hope to include in this number which we expect to be able to increase to twelve pages. Violet returns to the fold in this number, and we will have to forgive her for her temporary desertion which she has explained prettily to us. We should now like to wish you one and all the best of luck at Xmas and during the coming year.

THE EDITOR.

BRAZIER PICTURES.

Christmastide, Christmastide, mistletoe
    and holly,
   Lovely girls and ingle nook
   Gaiety where'er you look
   In each magazine or book
    Banish melancholy.

—:o:—

   In my brazier as I gaze
   Pictures come and pictures go,
   Dimly seen across the haze—
   Christmases we used to know.

—:o:—

Now the coals burn clear and bright
   There I see a merry throng
   Round the fire, one Xmas night,
   Laughter ringing loud and long.

—:o:—

   Now the glow has disappeared,
   And my dug-out's overcast,
   Just outside the night is seared
   With a shell, or Minnie's blast,

—:o:—

Now again she's burning clear,
   Visions come of better days,
   Gone discomforts that are near,
   Hope around my dug-out plays.

—:o:—

   Pictures come and pictures go,
   Yet one truth alone remains,
   He who strikes the best last blow,
   He it is the prize who gains.,

—:o:—

   So what matter mud or snow?
   Spring and Summer come in turn,
   Better days will come, and so
   Burn, my good old brazier, burn.

GONE.

Gone are the days of the Seventythird,
  When never a quail or a grouse was
      heard,
Gone are our smiles—each eye has a tear
For gone is our priceless Brigadier;
We ne'er shall forget his cheery face,
Tho' we've got another to take his place.

—§ † §—

Gone is the Transport Officer too
" Dear old Charles " whom all ranks
      knew,
Knocked out by a shell for a Bosch who
      flew,
They say that the air for miles went blue;
We ne'er shall forget his cheery face,
Tho' we've got another to take his place.

—§ † §—

Gone half of the firm who advertise,
He never again will dazzle our eyes
With the wonderful cap, with its band so
      red,
He wore on the back of his curly head;
We ne'er shall forget his cheery face,
Tho' we've got another to take his place.

—§ † §—

But there's still one left of the old
      Brigade,
Who always pretends he's old and staid,
He teaches the new ones how to go
In the ways of the others we used to
      know;
We ne'er shall forget his cheery face,
And want no other to take his place.

—§ † §—

They've not gone far, and we hope some
      day
To meet 'em again when we're all at play,
When the Huns have gone where all
      Huns should be,
And we're playing at soldiers near
      Camberley;
To chin of the things we have seen and
      heard
And the things we did in the Seventy-
      third.

                T. G.

RATS.

I want to write a poem, yet I find I have
no theme,
" Rats " are no subject for an elegy,
Yet they fill my waking moments, and
when star-shells softly gleam,
'Tis the rats who spend the midnight
hours with me.

—o—o—o—

On my table in the evening they will
form " Battalion mass,"
They will open tins of bully with their
teeth,
And should a cake be sent me by some
friend at home, alas !
They will extricate it from its cardboard
sheath.

—o—o—o—

They are bloated, fat and cunning, and
they're marvels as to size,
And their teeth can penetrate a sniping
plate,
I could tell you tales unnumbered, but
you'd think I'm telling lies,
Of one old, grey whiskered buck-rat and
his mate.

—o—o—o—

Just to show you, on my table lay a tin
of sardines—sealed—
With the implement to open hanging
near,
The old buck-rat espied them, to his
missis loudly squealed,
" Bring quickly that tin-opener, Stinky
dear ! "

—o—o—o—

She fondly trotted up the pole, and
brought him his desire,
He proceeded then with all his might
and main,
He opened up that tin, and then—'tis
here you'll dub me " Liar ! "—
He closed it down, and sealed it up again.

—o—o—o—

Have you seen one, should a rival chance
to spoil his love affair,
Bring a bomb, Mills, hand, and place it
underneath
The portion of the trench where that said
rival had his lair,
And then he'll pull the pin out with his
teeth.

OUR SHORT STORY.

—:0:—

It was Xmas morning in the trenches !
M-m-m-m-m.

Peace, peace, let us have peace,
Quoth Bill with a face grave and long ;
You can see we have won
Ere you've really begun,
So let's chuck it while I'm going strong.

INTELLIGENCE.

SUMMARY MEASURES.

" O " the Observer who stood at his post,
And at 3 on the 10th saw a small German
host
Going East with a cart, so he had a good
look,
And proceeded to make—a note in his
book.

—:o:—

" D " the Division who read the next day
The report " O " had rendered, and sent
it away
To Corps, where it rested, until bye-and-
bye
The Army decided that those Huns
should die.

—:o:—

So a mandate was issued to Corps as a
start,
To slaughter those Huns going East with
a cart,
Which mandate was then with decision
and ease
Pushed on to Division, "for action please.

—:o:—

Division post-haste, or as near as could be,
Sent word to the gunners of what " O "
could see,
The gunners prepared with shot and with
shell,
To blow those said Germans from here
into Hell.

—:o:—

With lanyard in hand, and with cool
flashing eye,
They scanned all the landscape, they
scanned all the sky—
And here we will leave them, gazing apart
For the Huns who—A WEEK AGO—passed
with a cart.

BY ORDER.

—o—o—

Oh dear! Nearly a column to be written, and the Editor has detailed me for the job. He won't have anything about the War, as he says he's "fed up" with that subject, so what on earth shall I yarn about? I wonder if he's heard the tale of the Transport Officer and the rum. Of course there are many tales of T.O.'s and rum. The oldest one of all is the one of the T.O. who didn't like rum. But this tale I'm going to tell you is true. There was once a T.O. who was coming up with the rations. The said rations included " rum for weary soldiers." Also the cargo had a consignment of tear-gas in a rum-jar for the M.O. to try a few experiments with. That is all the tale—but I may as well add that the T.O. recovered. Did you ever hear the tale of the General, the Tommy, and the letter. Oh! I mustn't tell that tale, what a pity! (I wonder how many tales it takes to fill a column.) Did you ever hear the tale of the five officers in a dug out? One I am afraid had too great a fancy for alcoholic stimulant. A great big fat rat appeared. Silently they all looked at one another. " I didn't see it ! " blurted out our alcoholic friend. That ought to about do it, so, having obeyed orders, I'm off to bed. Adios !

AUNT ANNIE'S CORNER.

TINY TALKS TO TINY TOTS.

MY Dear Lit-tle Tot-ties, It is a long time since I have been able to an-swer your nice lit-tle let-ters, for your Aunt'ie has been bus-y. Clev-er Tot-ties will know what bus-y means. It means your poor Aunt-ie has had to WORK. Work is a hor-rid thing, and I am sure my Tot-ties never have anything to do with it, do they? Some of my Tot-ties have writ-ten me lit-tle let-ters all about Christ-mas. Here are the ans-wers to them.

DEAR Buf-fy, It was so nice of your friends to lend you all their sol-diers to play with. Per-haps one day Santa Claus will put a lot in your stock-ing of your very own. That will be nice, won't it? And you must be careful not to break them. I hear you have been to school too. I hope you were a good boy.

DEAR little Mor-ice, I am sorry Santa Claus made such a silly mistake, and put some curl-ing tongs in your stock-ing. Never mind, you will be able to give them to your lit-tle friend Ken-neth. He will be pleased. I am glad you have a nice new red hat. Also you tell me you are fond of dogs. That is kind of you..

DEAR Rog-er, I am sorry you have been ra-ther un-well late-ly, but I hope you are bet-ter now. You did not tell me what Santa Claus put in your stock-ing, but I hope it was some-thing nice. Have you been for any long walks late-ly? I am glad you are going to have a par-ty. That will be nice, and all your lit-tle friends will en-joy it very much. You must be pol-ite to them, and show them your new pic-tures.

Good-bye, Tot-ties,
Your Ev-er Dov-ing
AUNT ANNIE.

OUR MATRIMONIAL COLUMN.

Everything in this department receives the greatest discretion and secrecy, and correspondents may be assured that all correspondence is treated with the utmost delicacy.

CAPTAIN.—35, handsome and dashing appearance. Thoroughly domesticated and capable of looking after the home. Feels lost in his present position of Camp Commandant. Fond of dogs. Would welcome correspondence with a view to matrimony. Money no object as he has his pay.—Write Vatican, c/o this paper.

BRIG GENERAL.—Young — charm-ing personality—feels lonely Bashful-ness has made him take this way of settling his future happiness, and he would like to correspond with some priceless· young lady matrimonially inclined.—Write Rudolph, c/o this paper.

BRIG. GENERAL. — Companiable—jocose—domesticated—loving. Is feeling his unattached condition very much, and seizes this opportunity of making over-tures to some sympathetic young lady. — Write Jock, c/o this paper.

LIEUT-COLONEL. — Gone grey through loneliness. Feels that his life could be brightened by the introduction of a female element. Romantic dis-positon, and has had many "affaires," but would entertain an opportunity of settling down Widow preferred. Money no object, but would like one with small public house.—Write Buffs, c/o this paper.

LIEUT.-COLONEL.—Tall and striking appearance. Just recovered from wound, feels lost now without feminine attentions, and would welcome correspondence that might ultimately end in providing him with congenial society for life.— Write Rugger, c/o this paper.

—:o:—

(Many thousand advertisements are held over for lack of space.)

Things We Want to Know.

—:o:—

What is the story about " Mother."

? ? ?

When is the regulation referring to hunting stocks and crops going to apply to shooting suits

? ? ?

The number of bones that have been sent to the soup kitchen up-to-date, and what is being done with them

? ? ?

The name of the motorist who has a passion for collecting cows on the Boulogne Road, and what the natives think of his pet hobby.

? ? ?

Whether a certain officer is shortly publishing a little song entitled " Why was I so careless with the boots."

? ? ?

Whether a Camp Commandant we know can give us a return of the number of dogs in his district size, colour and pedigree.

? ? ?

Whether the new collection of Old Masters at the Munque Art Gallery doesn't beat the old one.

VIOLET'S CHRONICLE OF FASHION.

(AND OTHER MATTERS.)

(SUBS. NOT TO READ THIS—ED.)

—o—o—o—

YOU have doubtless heard of the sub. who defined a lady as one who wears stockings that are silk all the way up (Which is perhaps hardly fair to those whose misplaced ideas of economy lead them to purchase what the shops call " silk-ankles.") Well, he will have to revise his definition, anyway. For not only our stockings must be silk nowadays, but all "les dessous." Never has lingerie been more fascinating,—or more extravagant ; but girls whose war-work prevents the wearing of pretty frocks may be forgiven if they indulge in frillies instead. Garments are fairy-like in their filmy beauty,—camisoles are airy fragments of chiffon, lace, and ribbon just blown together, petticoats are real poems, while as for night-wear, even the simplest designs are artistic triumphs, and the materials are so dainty and sometimes so diaphanous that the result seems a mere ghost of a nightie !

DANCES still flourish down in "our village," much to the joy of the inhabitants of the local camps. The boys of one regiment have earned our gratitude by bringing over their own band, for it's getting difficult to find a good orchestra ; think we shall have to give other regiments a hint to do likewise, the invitations might conclude " Pretty partners provided, but bring your own music." It is nice to see those same partners as the most charming butterflies imaginable at night, for nearly all are the busiest of bees by day. We appreciate our gaieties now, after hours of sewing at a depôt, serving at a canteen, making shells, or minding babies while their mothers make them !

A PARAGRAPH in my last chronicle concerning officers who invite me to lunch promptly brought me a letter from friend "Sabretâche." He wrote me that I "must NOT go out with any of those soldier devils—one never knows !" Well, advice from a man like "Sabretâche" is not to be ignored, and he will be pleased to know that I have obediently refused all luncheon invitations, and gone to dinner instead every time.

VIOLET.

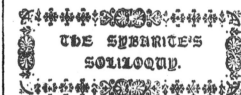

THE SYBARITE'S SOLILOQUY.

Dearest, at break of Dawn, I need you most,
And, as you, in your silver shrouded dress,
Gambol before my eyes, I daily bless
The coins that made you mine, the trifling cost,
That sold you into bondage, such as this ;
To be my Slave, Enchantress of my Soul,
To pay, afresh, each morn, the levied toll,
That I extort from you—a honied kiss.
And, as, upon my cheeks, my rugged chin,
Your scented lips, you passionately press,
In muscadine abandon, I caress
Your adipose delight, and with a grin,
Each morning, half awake, for you, I grope
Oh Stick of Superfatted Shaving Soap.

C. L. P.

Mr. Teech Bomas.

—o—o—o—

We regret to inform our readers that as Mr. TEECH BOMAS has left for his usual winter trip to warmer climes, all proceedings will be stopped meanwhile. The battle will be resumed immediately on his return, when we hope to have further graphic articles from his pen. —ED.

FAREWELL.

—:o:—

We have been asked, by many of his friends in the Division, to say good-bye to Brig.-General Jelf for them through our columns. His old Brigade feels his departure acutely. It is no reflection on our new Brigadier to say that he will have a hard job to occupy the place held by General Jelf in the hearts of all ranks, who one and all knew him for a chum. We wish him a speedy recovery, and he will know that he carries with him all our wishes for his future success, and refer him to the last verse of " Gone " in this number.

Here also we should like to extend a hearty welcome to our new Brigadier, and to express our conviction that his popularity will equal that of his predecessor. " Le roi est mort, vive le Roi." THE EDITOR.

Correspondence.

To the Editor,
    " B.E.F. Times."
Sir,
    May I ask for the assistance of your widely read columns to further the interests of a much neglected charity. I refer to the fund for providing flannel pyjamas for our troops in the front line. We hear on reliable authority that these poor fellows are very short of pyjamas, and in many cases have only one pair. Surely something can be done to help them in this matter. We were so successful with our fund for providing " Umbrellas for our gallant sailors," that we have great hopes of our new appeal. All contributions must be sent to the secretary.
    I am, Sir,
        Yours faithfully,
            ELIZA STIGGINS, Hon Sec.

Printed &
Published by
Sherwood, Forester &
Co , Ltd.
B.F. F.

THE

B. E. F. TIMES.

WITH WHICH ARE INCORPORATED

The Wipers Times, The "New Church" Times,
The Kemmel Times & The Somme-Times.

No 3.　Vol 1.　　　　Saturday January 20th, 1917.　　　Price 1 Franc.

EDITORIAL.

 JANUARY 1st, 1917. Here's the best of luck for the New Year to all our readers. Whatever it may have in store for us, we can at least be thankful we are not Huns. If they were anyone else but Huns one might feel sorry for them, and send them a card of sympathy for the trouble in store. If we were Old Moore, and gifted with prophetic insight, we would go as far to make a note in our diary, " 1917—Disturbances in Europe " However, we will leave prophecy to those who understand tactics, etc., and Major Taude, B.C may be induced to send us an article on " What the Germans will do in 1917." There also we could sum the matter up briefly by saying, " Get it where the bottle got the cork," but we prefer to have the matter more eloquently expressed by him. We have now completed our first year of journalism, and are feeling quite old hands at the game, talking learnedly of " dis-ing " and chases, furniture, etc. It was certainly a lucky day for us when we found the old " Jigger," otherwise we should have been hard put to it to fill in all the spare time which we have on our hands during these pleasant winter months. Talking of Winter we are of the opinion that it should change places with Autumn and be called the " Fall." Personally we think there's a lot too much fall about it. We are often glad to be able to think we are only soldiering for pleasure. It would be terrible to think that we HAD to do it. Well! We are getting through the Winter somehow, and soon shall be thinking of Spring. " In the Spring a young man's fancy lightly turns to thoughts of —" grenades, hand, Mills and any other lethal article he can lay his hands on. America seems to abound in humourists, and President Wilson is rather undermining Mark Twain's reputation· A new edition of "The Innocents Abroad" from the pen of the gifted President would be certain of instant success. As we are writing a terrible rumour has reached us, that whiskey will shortly be "na-poo." This is the most unkindest cut of all, and as the sub-editor crudely puts it "No whiskey, no war." Can anyone imagine calling at the "Culvert Arms" and being told that whiskey was "Off." Good Heavens! It will be the ruin of many a good old-established house, and we should not be surprised if many of the most popular dug-outs in the line had to shut their gas-curtains. However, all this and more we will bear for England's sake, but it is going to be a dry summer. We must request all competitors in our new Competition not to go in massed formation to search for the buried cheques as it inconveniences the Hun. Sections of ten at 50 yards interval would be advisable, and we wish to state here that the Menin Road East of the Culvert Arms is closed to all vehicular traffic including buses. As our previous appeals have met with very little response we should like to make a fresh effort and remind all readers that copy is urgently required if we are to keep up to 12 pages, and beg one and all to send something along. Once more wishing you all the best of luck during 1917.

THE EDITOR.

Let me like a soldier fall,
  Upon an open plain ;
For if I trip and fall in a trench,
  I could never get up again

There was a little Hun, and at war he
    tried his hand,
And while that Hun was winning war
    was fine you understand,
But when the others hit him back he
    shouted in alarm,
A little drop of peace wouldn't do me
    any harm.

TO MY MARRAINE.

I love you for your kindliness and grace,
And wonder how it happens, that you
    deign
To send me sweets and gifts, my dear
    MARRAINE,
Across the intervening miles of space
Your portrait, in the evening mists, I
    trace,
While doing sentry, in the mud and
    rain,
The sky is dark above ; but free from
    stain
Or blemish, is your lovely visioned face.

—o—o—o—

However long this war goes on. MARRAINE,
I'll love you, I'll adore you, to the end ;
But all the Doctor's Magic cannot shake
From my inside, this unaccustomed
    pain,
I pray you, I implore you, not to send
Another sanguinary HOME-MADE cake.

THE M.O. (C.L.P.)

DISTURBING INFLUENCES.

In dug-out cool I sit and freeze as on
  the war I ponder,
My thoughts on Huns and guns don't
  please, and so begin to wander,
Green fields, and peace, and lovely girls,
  or in my club I'm drinking,
When outside—bang—and of the war,
  I'm thinking, thinking, thinking,

I freely curse the blighted Hun who
  interrupts my fancies,
And with his frightfulness breaks in on
  memoried romances ;
No Wilson I, nor has my pen much skill
  in temporisals,
So naught is left for me to do, save swift
  T.M. reprisals.

I hate all Huns, yet most hate I, that
  surly livered blighter,
Who with persistence breaks my sleep,
  with his ten times-a-nighter ;
When fast asleep, and in the arms of
  Morpheus or some other,
The rotter looses off and then—oh,
  damn it, there's another

Yet I will wait, and patiently, to catch
  the blighter bending,
And constantly unto my aid will summon
  guns unending ;
With six-inch Hows, and every kind of
  gun will wreck his dwelling,
And when we'll hold his requiem mass,
  our Stokes shall do his knelling.

RHYMES WITHOUT REASON.

BY P.B.I.

FOREWORD.

—o—

Arise, My MUSE, and from the muddied
trench
Let us give utterance to malicious
thought,
Shouting aloud the things we never ought
Even to dream of : come, you shameless
Wench,
With tongue in cheek let us set out to
strafe
Gunners and Sappers, and the Gilded
Staff.

— o—o—o —

(I.)

Gunners are a race apart.
Hard of head and hard of heart.
Like the gods they sit and view
All that other people do :
Like the Sisters Three of Fate,
They do not discriminate.
Our Support Line, or the Hun's,
—What's the difference to the Guns ?
Retaliation do you seek ?
Ring them up, and—wait a week !
They will certainly reply
In the distant by-and-bye.
Should a shell explode amiss,
Each will swear it was not his :
For he's never, never shot
Anywhere about that spot,
And, what's more, his Guns could not.

(II.)

Sappers are wonderfully clever by birth,
And though they're not meek, they
inherit the Earth.
Should your trenches prove leaky, they'll
work with a will
To make all the water flow up the next
hill
(And when I say "work," I should
really explain
That we find the Labour, while they find
the Brain).
They build nice, deep dug-outs as quick
as can be,
But quicker still mark them "RESERVED
FOR R.E." :
And, strangely, this speed of theirs
seems to decline
As the scene of their labours draws near
the Front Line.

—o—o—o—

(III.)

Realising Men must laugh,
Some Wise Man devised the Staff :
Dressed them up in little dabs
Of rich variegated tabs :
Taught them how to win the War
On A.F.Z. 354 :
Let them lead the Simple Life
Far from all our vulgar strife :
Nightly gave them downy beds
For their weary, aching heads :
Lest their relatives might grieve
Often, often, gave them leave,
Decorations, too, galore :
What on earth could man wish more ?
Yet, alas, or so says Rumour,
He forgot a sense of Humour !

—o—o—o—

AFTERWORD.

—o—

And now, Old Girl, we've fairly had our
whack,
Be off, before they start to strafe us back !
Come, let us plod across the weary Plain,
Until we sight TENTH AVENUE again :
On, up the interminable C.T.,

Watched by the greater part of Germany:
And, as we go, mark each familiar
    spot.
Where fresh work has been done—or
    p'r'aps has not :
On, past the footboards no one seems to
    mend,
Till even VENDIN ALLEY finds an end,
And wading through a Minnie-hole
    (brand-new),
We gingerly descend to C.H.Q.,
Our journey ended in a Rabbit-hutch—
" How goes the Battle ? Have they
    Minnied much ? "

            P.B.1.

Things We Want to Know.

—:o:—

The name of the Camp Commandant
who bought up all the whiskey in
Bethune owing to early advice of the
coming drought.

     ? ? ?

The name of the M.O. who is not a
doctor.

     ? ? ?

If it is true that he takes an umbrella
on his walks, as " Archie " duds are so
plentiful.

     ? ? ?

Whether two notorious red-hats were
disappointed over a little question of
" Who's HE taking with him."

     ? ? ?

Ref. G.R.O. Q.M.G.'s Branch No.
2073 :—(A)—What is a BONA FIDE rum
drinker. (B)—Whether whiskey cannot
be supplied on the same terms to BONA
FIDE whiskey drinkers.

AN APPEAL.

There are various types of courage, there
    are many kinds of fear,
There are many brands of whiskey, there
    are many makes of beer,
There is also rum, which sometimes in
    our need can help us much,
But 'tis whiskey—whiskey—whiskey !
    hands the courage which is "Dutch."

In moments when the front is still—no
    hustling whizzbangs fly—
In all the world you could not find a
    braver man than I !
Yet on patrol in No-Man's-Land, when
    I may have to stalk a
Benighted Hun, in moments tense I
    have recourse to " Walker."

'Tis Scotland's best which helps me rest,
    'tis Mountain Dew which stays me
When Minnies rack my wearied soul, or
    blatant H.E. flays me,
'Twas by its aid that I endured Trones
    Wood and such-like places.
In times of stress my truest friend accel-
    erates my paces.

Take what you will save only this—my
    evening tot of whiskey,
It gives me warmth, and helps to make
    a soaking much less risky,
Oh ! G.O.C.'s now hear our pleas
    respectfully presented,
Lend us your aid in this our plight, and
    we will be contented.

        ONE & ALL.

AN APPEAL.

There are various types of courage, there
    are many kinds of fear,
There are many brands of whiskey, there
    are many makes of beer,
There is also rum, which sometimes in
    our need can help us much,
But 'tis whiskey—whiskey—whiskey !
    hands the courage which is "Dutch."

In moments when the front is still—no
    hustling whizzbangs fly—
In all the world you could not find a
    braver man than I !
Yet on patrol in No-Man's-Land, when
    I may have to stalk a
Benighted Hun, in moments tense I
    have recourse to " Walker."

'Tis Scotland's best which helps me rest,
    'tis Mountain Dew which stays me
When Minnies rack my wearied soul, or
    blatant H.E. flays me,
'Twas by its aid that I endured Trones
    Wood and such-like places.
In times of stress my truest friend accel-
    erates my paces.

Take what you will save only this—my
    evening tot of whiskey,
It gives me warmth, and helps to make
    a soaking much less risky,
Oh ! G.O.C.'s now hear our pleas
    respectfully presented,
Lend us your aid in this our plight, and
    we will be contented.

            ONE & ALL.

AUNT ANNIE'S CORNER.

—o—o—o—

TENDER TALKS TO TINY TOTS.

—o—o—

MY Dear Lit-tle Tot-ties,
          Your poor
Auntie has so many let-ters from her
dear lit-tle Tot-ties that she can-not
ans-wer them all this week, but she will
talk to you about some of them. Two
of my Tot-ties are very sad, and they
want me to tell them what to do.

—:o:—

POOR Lit-tle Gun-ner had a love-ly
    pair of breech-es given to him, but
a nasty boy took them and hid them.
When he told the other boys about it
they all laugh-ed at him and said that
Mother had tak en them a-way from him.
He says that the other boys laugh
be-cause he likes to wear some pretty
toy spurs. Ar'n't they hor-rid boys ?
Well, Gunner, do not be sad, the other
boys only laugh be-cause they have not
got such nice breech-es and spurs. They
are jeal-ous.

—:o:—

THE other sad Tot-tie is lit-tle Rabs.
    He makes nice tren-ches, and the
naught-y rain comes and wash-es them
a-way. He says it is a pity, as he does
not often work. Well, Rabs, don't be
down-heart-ed (isn't that a big word
Tot-ties ?), if you keep on and work
hard-er, some day you will get something done. You must not take any
not-ice of the big pi-on-eers who you
say laugh at you, and it was not nice of
you to put out your tongue at them. My
Tot-ties do not do that.

—:o:—

LIT-TLE Mike Bell tells me he has
    gone to live in a new place with
the big boys, and has a nice new hat, a
red one, and a nice coat with a red
col-lar. Isn't he a luck-y boy, Tot-ties ?
I hope he will re-mem-ber all the nice
things we taught him.

—:o:—

    Good-bye Tot-ties, be good,
        Your Loving
            AUNT ANNIE.

A PLEA FROM THE TRENCHES.

—:o:—

EXTRACT FROM "DAILY SKETCH,"
JANUARY 2ND, 1917.

—:o:—

MAKING THE TRENCHES "COMFY."

—:o:—

"The mothers, sisters and sweethearts of the men in the trenches will be delighted to hear of the latest instance of the solicitude of the military chiefs for their comfort and good health. Every yard of roofing felt that can be found in the United Kingdom is being commandeered for the lining of the trenches on the Western Front. It is sound policy as well as strong sentiment which is at the back of such wise provision."

Mr. GOSSIP.

—o—o—

Dear Mr. Gossip,—

This is really splendid reading that you have given us. Now we shall be able to carry on with no fear of the future. The lack of lining in our trenches has been the one dark spot in our existence. How often we have sat on our well-aired beds and regretted the fact that we had no roofing felt to line our trenches, while only last week one of my Sergeants' asked me to indent for two or three miles, but knowing the cheese-paring policy of Q.M's I refrained. Do you think the Government will follow this up to its legitimate conclusion? You see the steps of our dugouts are so bare, and if only it were properly represented to them, the Government might be persuaded to buy up all the carpet and send it over. It would be so nice if our "Mothers, sisters and sweethearts" could think of us going up and down our nicely carpeted steps. Also may I bring to your notice the shameful way we are treated in the trenches themselves. We have to walk on bare duckboards, (my pal Bill got corns on his feet through having to do this) surely we might be provided with linoleum. I put these suggestions forward in a tentative manner, and if you can do anything for us in the matter we should be so obliged. It would give such joy to our "Mothers, sisters and sweethearts." I have only mentioned essentials, such things as curtains for our dug outs, draught-preventors for the doors, and door-mats with "Welcome" on will come later. Do help us for we cannot help ourselves."

"ONE SPOT."

B.E.F. GAZETTE,
January 1st, 1917.

—:o:—

We are pleased to be able to state that a large and assorted collection of orders from foreign potentates has been received and the Division comes in for a good share. They have been allotted thus :—

To be High Sheik of the Order of the " Numero Neuf."

The A.D.M.S

—:o:—

To be Commander of the Order of the " Piebald Foal or Fatted Calf."

The A.D.V S.

—:o:—

To be Knight Commander of the Most Ancient Order of the " Magdalenes."

The A.P.M.

—:o:—

To be Companion of the Order of the " Rising Sun."

The B.M . rd I.B.

—:o: -

To be High Sheriff of the Most Noble Legion of " Kew Wemms."

The D.A.D.O.S.

—:o:—

The Expanded Medal.

The O.C., Field Coy.

Correspondence.

To the Editor,
"B.E.F. Times."

Sir,

The other evening while taking a stroll through the system of canals which festoon the district, I called at the local soup kitchen, thinking that a cup of hot refreshing soup would compensate me for having missed my evening tot of rum. I was here met with a query as to how a perspiring and angry individual could "Supply the bloomin' Harmy wi' soup, when all he could find was a couple er dead Huns, and well scraped bone, and turnip tops?" Can nothing be done?

INDIGNANS.

—o—o—o—

To the Editor,
"B.E.F. Times."

Sir,

I am a brain worker to whom peace and quiet are a necessity. After moving my quarters many times, I, at length, found a district which seemed to possess those advantages. I WAS MISTAKEN. Shortly after taking up my residence here a "lady" (of whose character the less said perhaps the better) has come to live opposite my house. I am no moralist, but I must protest against the noises in the street caused either by the "lady" herself or by persons interested in her. The "lady" I believe is known as "Minnie." Can nothing be done to move, or at least to have her kept quiet?

I am, sir,
Yours Faithfully,
"PAX."

—o—o—o—

To the Editor.
"B.E.F. Times."

Sir,

As I was going over the top last week I distinctly heard the call of the cuckoo. I claim to be the first to have heard it this spring, and should like to know if any of your readers can assert that they heard it before me.

I am, sir,
Yours Faithfully,
A "LOVER OF NATURE."

(That ought to about settle it for this year.—ED.)

To the Editor,
"B.E.F. Times."

Sir,

As one of the oldest inhabitants of our pretty little village, may I protest very strongly against the noisy behaviour of the new arrivals. So strongly have I the welfare of my fellow citizens at heart that I mean to be quite frank. The worst offender is Doctor Squiller, whose children are continually playing with the most noisy toys, the worst being a particularly blatant pop-gun. Surely the idyllic happiness of our little township should not be spoilt by such hooliganisms.

I am, etc.,
A PEACEFUL MAN.

(The question of street noises is rapidly becoming a nuisance, and the City Fathers must be brought to realise their responsibilities.—ED. "B.E.F. Times.")

ANSWERS TO CORRESPONDENTS.

ANXIOUS   Your answer to "Vatican's" matrimonial advertisement will doubtless be replied to in due course. You must understand that "Vatican" is so snowed up with applications for his hand that he cannot deal with them all at once. Besides he is a red-hat, and MAY have other work to do.

ENQUIRER.—No. Two sandbags and one sheet of corrugated iron will NOT as a rule keep out a 5·9. We should advise you to consult Mr. Blewes, the well-known expert.

THE
B. E. F. TIMES.

WITH WHICH ARE INCORPORATED

The Wipers Times, The "New Church" Times, The Kemmel Times & The Somme-Times.

No 4. Vol I.   Monday, March 5th, 1917.   Price 1 Franc.

EDITORIAL.

SPRING is co-o-o-o-ming! Can you imagine the blithesome Hun sticking his head out of a dug-out and surveying with any pleasure the prospect of a dawning Spring? Winter's snowy mantle has gone, and in its place we have several feet of Belgium's best. The M.O. tells me that he has noticed on several occasions lately the development of web-feet in some of his clientéle. The M.O. having some slight reputation for veracity (perhaps more traditional than actual) one must accept what he says, and wonder how it is all going to end. One contributor in the last number seems to have drawn the gunners fire, but the red-hats remain still distant and 'aloof, ignoring the gibes of less-effulgent people. We really must congratulate the B.E.F. on the success of the War Loan, but feel sure we can beat 800,000,000 next time, and still save a bit out of our pay. Having lately been on leave we have had a good opportunity of learning how things are going on the Western Front. One cannot help feeling surprised at the obviously enormous amount of military genius allowed to run spare owing to a unobservant and decadent Government. We must express the regret that is felt generally. at the departure of so many of the old crowd for newer and larger fields of activity. Of course it is nice to feel that most of the stars of the Army come from the Division yet one misses their cheery faces. It is obvious from some of the efforts submitted recently that there is plenty of talent in the Division, and so we can look confidently forward to the future, and feel assured we shall be able to keep up to twelve pages.

The lengthy instalment of the Serial in this number is attributable to the fact that we turned it over to a subaltern with ideas. SOME ideas, you will agree, and it will be interesting to see what he's going to do with the central characters taking a toss in an aeroplane. Truth is stranger than fiction. We have come to the conclusion that we shall either have to give up the war or the editorial chair. The sub editor has just remarked that if that's so we'd better give up the war as no one would notice it. That is only the bitterness of a disappointed man, and probably arises from a temporary severance of diplomatic relations with Messrs. Cox and Co. But, seriously! What a country! One writes nice things about the disappearance of winter's snowy mantle, and then it goes back on you and starts all over again. We must thank the few of the Division who have sent us copy, and ask the many who have Something for the paper," to jot it down in writing and send it along, as often, after a long round of visiting, all the anecdotes retailed to the Editor en route sort of get mixed up together, and much that would have been useful gets lost in transit. Greetings to all.

THE EDITOR.

If I were King! Ah! Bill, if I were King,
I wouldn' touch an "A" frame or a thing,
I'd watch the sergeant split his blooming thumb,
And, when he wasn't looking, drink his rum,
I'd make the corpr'l rations to me bring,
If I were King! Ah! Bill, if I were King.

TO MELT A STONE.

Kindly manager of Cox,
I am sadly on the rocks,
For a time my warring ceases,
My patella is in pieces ;
Though in Hospital I lie,
I am not about to die ;
Therefore let me overdraw
Just a very little more,
If you stick to your red tape
I must go without my grape,
And my life must sadly fret
With a cheaper cigarette,
So pray be not hard upon
A poor dejected subaltern,
This is all I have to say,

"IMPECUNIOUS," R.F.A.

ALLEGED ANSWER FROM COX'S.

—o—o—o—

Sir, the kindly heart of Cox
Cannot leave you on the rocks,
And he could not sleep in bed
Thinking you were underfed ;
So if you will let us know
Just how far you want to go,
Your request will not be vain,
Written from your bed of pain,
We will make but one request—
Keep this locked within your breast,
For if others know, they'll say,
" Good old Cox is sure to pay,
Only take him the right way."
(Note.—This opens up new vistas.
—ED.)

A VOUS.

Here, in these sunny southern climes
  (Its pelting in Milan this minute)
It reaches me—our " Wipers Times "
And idly I peruse what's in it :
Till, through the clanging of the trams
That thread the snow where beauty
                              flounders,
I hear the crash of British damns,
The roar of British eighteen-pounders,
And live once more in savage North
Where life is wet, and wierd, and risky,
One of that gallant ' twenty-fourth '—
And drink once more the Sherwoods
                              whisky ;
And meet the friends I used to meet,
Gunner and P.B.I. and Sapper,
When sweet was ration rum, and sweet
The work we did for General Capper .
Alas, those days are done, in place
Of German shells and brass-hats'
                              strictures.
Armed to the teeth, I sternly face
Your war . . . . as shown in moving
                              pictures !
Here Marchesine (save the mark
Strafe loudly on that grand piano !)
Divinely tall, divinely dark,
Smile on an English Capitano,
Who wears a sword, and spotless breeks,
And spurs would make a hairy tremble.
And plays the hero stunt . . . and shrieks
With laughter he can scarce dissemble
For this you know, old comrades, tried
To breaking-point of e en your humour,
That never since de Rougemont died
Was hero such a perfect ' stumer.'
You know, who tramped the Menin
                              Road,
And visited the Culvert nightly
That I, your bard who pens this ode,
Ne'er left his crump-proof dug-out
                              lightly,

But slaked the thirst of martial ire,
To his own utter satisfaction,
With miles of buried D.5 wire
And chits he 'passed to you for action'.
Which being so, pray you that fight
In trenches where is no steam-heating
Accept from me, your bard, to-night,
A very humble New Year's greeting.

GILBERT FRANKAU

Telegraphic address : —
  Movie-King, Italy.

THE LEAVE WARRANT

Week, after weary week, I work and wait
Patiently wondering, when 'twill be my
                              lot
To find a carpet, wond'rously wrought
On mystic looms, in some enchanted
                              state,
Gifted with Oriental power innate
To bear me hence, to other lands, I wot
(In dreams, I sit upon it, but do not
Awake in time to ring the bell of Fate)
But willingly, indeed, I would forego
This Magic Mat, for just a little bit
Of printed, primrose parchment—and to
                              know,
That on its face my name three times
                              was writ.
For 'tis a genie's golden key to fit
The Gate of Leave—" Chin chin, you
                              chaps, cheer O ! "

                              C.L.P.

THE BACK.

—o—o—o—

As the Front is left behind, the inner meaning of the war becomes more apparent. The elusive Adjutant and the bashful R.S.M. resume their true importance in our lives, as they emerge from their hiding places: Town Majors, A.P.M.'s, Quartermasters, Mice Officers, Instructors, Lecturers, Missionaries, Experts, Staff Officers, all become like common hedgerow flowers in Springtime: and I have known a man who had seen a stray hothouse seedling from G.H.Q., but he told me the yarn in the early hours after his first bottle of O.O., when the Inland Water Transport fellow was short circuited. The further back you get the nearer you get to that spot where all the "Paper" comes from, which I will tell you about in letters of blood-red in the next number. Buy it for your unborn children: the horror of going there will keep them always good. However, I am very happy, thank you. At the moment I live on a range where there are far more rounds per day fired in anger than in the line. Repairs prove that. Still the range is the envy of those not using it. I know that, because Lewis gunners, bombers, rifle grenadiers, and musketry recruits all like, from a flank and rear position, to get as near our targets as they can: probably from a kindly desire to increase the number of hits on them. The Range Officer has a most enviable job in this little backwater of life.

It is truly a backwater with the water always backing up and defeating the working parties, and one well-read Hophni told me he always called the place Aaron's Range, because his rod had done its work so well.

A morning quickly passes in such light and refreshing work as picking up the chocolate tin-foil and paper of the previous day's firing party, helping up a refractory target constructed in the best R.E. manner, strafing about the empty cartridge cases, opening up a drain, visiting sentries and explaining to them that it really is not part of their duty to look death in the face by walking about in rear of the stop butt etc.: in fact one is quite surprised when the first party moves off hurling anathemas owing to enforced fatigues, and one is at last alone with the meagre unexpended portion of the previous day's ration in one hand and a fat flask in the right, a true horn of plenty.

And at the end of a perfect day the parties shore off happily to their billets, and shortly to the joys of the line, and I to the bosom of my —[I beg your pardon, nothing of the sort: I forgot: I AM STILL B.E.F.]

GRANDPA.

To Fill a Column.

—o—o—o—

I can't think of any good tales to tell you. Of course there's the tale of the Brigadier and the Padre, but I suppose you've all heard that. Anyway both fell ill of the flue, and were straightway tucked away into beds in the same room. The Brigadier's tales were spicy, and the Padre was very unresponsive. Both, acting independently, surreptitiously sent for their clothes. Then, in rapid succession they approached the M.O. in charge and told him that, as they felt so much better, they were off. The Editor is sitting with a towel round his head, thinking hard. He doesn't know whether, on account of the increase in the price of paper, to double the price of this journal, or reduce the size. The Northcliffe bunch, by an effort of superb patriotism has doubled the price of their efforts. Hence the Editor's dilemma Wait and see.

A "B.-E.-F." ALPHABET.

A is the ARMY, in which he's a veteran
 Who's fought for a year from the
  Somme up to Meteren,
Finding in Winter each week is a wetter
   'un
And passing his days in the trenches.

B for old BLIGHTY, where, so we
   hear,
Prices are rising, and food is so dear
That a 'sub' can't afford to even go
   near :
It is cheaper to stay in the trenches.

C for the CAVALRY who, (so I've
   heard say)
Have not seen their gee-gees for many a
   day,
But soon they will mount them and
   gallop away,
And we'll all say good-bye to the trenches.

D for the DUCKBOARDS—if placed
   end to end
They'd girdle the Earth, and to Heaven
   ascend,
But I notice they've caused a peculiar
   blend
Of language to thrive in the trenches.

E for the EDITOR, ruddy in hue,
 He'd blue-pencil this if I said all I
   knew,
So I'll wish him good luck or—between
   me and you—
He'll send me exploring Hun trenches.

F for the FLYING CORPS—here we
   express
Our admiration : could we do less ?
They often have helped us out of a mess,
 "Cheer-oh !" from the men in the
   trenches.

G for the poisonous GAS that's emitted
 By fighters behind the line only
   half-witted,
But very pugnacious, and much to be
   pitied
By those who live in the trenches.

H for the HUN who lives over the way:
His future is black and his present
is grey :
Yet a Hun is a Hun, and as such he
must pay
For making us live in the trenches.

I for the INFANTRY prefixed "P.B.,"
One bob per diem and milk in their
tea :
They work day and night, after which
they are free
To start on a job in the trenches.

J for the JAR—if its contents are rum
A welcome awaits it whene'er it may
come :
Be it soon, be it late, there will always
be some
To greet it with joy in the trenches.

K'S for the KULTUR beneficent Huns
Endeavour to force down our
throats with big guns :
They send shells in packets, they send
them in ones :
But Kultur's Nar-Poo in the trenches.

L is for LEAVE, our goal of desire,
Ten days in Blighty away from the
mire
Hope springs eternal, and ne'er will
expire
In the breast of the men in the trenches.

M stands for MINNIE, whose shriek
rends the night :
They say that her bark is much worse
than her bite,
And if you can dodge her you'll sure be
all right :
But she isn't much loved in the trenches.

N for the NOMINAL ROLLS we send
through
Daily and weekly and monthly to 'Q' :
But we'd do it gladly and much worse
things too,
To finish the war in the trenches,

O the OBSERVER, who sees many
sights,
Such as stout German generals dancing
in tights,
And performing the most inexplicable
rites,
From his O-Pip in one of our trenches.

P'S for PEDICULI, horrible pests,
They make themselves happy in
trousers and vests ;
Though dear little fellows, they're un-
welcome guests
To the P.B.I. in the trenches.

Q? Well its obvious who fills this
place—
Princes of paper, the pride of our race—
Every movement and minute be sure
they can trace
And send back to the man in the trenches.

R the RETURNS to be rendered by
noon
Of the number of men who have seen a
blue moon,
Speak Japanese, or have been to Rangoon,
Before they came out to the trenches.

S for the SAPPERS, who sin without
shame,
And in spite of all efforts will go down
to fame
As the men who invented the five-bob
"A" frame,

T for the TRENCHES themselves (this
is where
I must take heed what I write, or I'll
swear!)
Which have blackened our souls, and
have whitened our hair :
Oh! Life is a dream in the trenches.

U for the UNIVERSE, whose fate 'tis
plain
Is now being settled in mud, slush and
rain,
By strafing which spreads from Nieuport
to Lorraine,
A line which is marked by our trenches.

V for the VICES soldiers posses,
Discovered by those who have been
more or less
Claimants to fame through a line in the
Press,
But never have shone in the trenches.

W for WHISKEY and WHIZZ-
BANGS as well :
Of the former I've almost forgotten the
smell,
Whilst the latter contribute to make it
like Hell
At various times in the trenches.

X for the unknown—and twixt you and
me
Fritz is now thinking (and we all agree)
That, hot as his present, his future will
be
Much hotter than e'er in the trenches.

Y for the YARNS that one hears—some
are true :
Others—Well! doubtless, though vivid
in hue,
Are spun by those ' back,' who have
never been through,
Or stood their whack of the trenches.

Z is for ZERO, the time we go over,
Most of us wish we were way back
in Dover,
Making munitions and living in clover
And far, far away from the trenches.

GOOD-BYE AND GOOD-LUCK.

ONCE again we say good bye to a Brigadier, this time to our oldest friend in the Division, Gen. B. MITFORD, C.B., D.S.O., who was with us in the beginning. What an age ago it seems now since a mob of aspiring and perspiring embryo soldiers used to perform wonderful feats under his skilful guidance on the Sussex Downs. How well we came to understand the terrors of war during those final rushes on Chanctonbury Ring! In addition to the regret of losing a Divisional friend, the editorial staff has also to mourn the loss of one of the first supporters and helpers of our paper. Gen. MITFORD assisted at the inception of the " Wipers Times," and has ever since given the greatest help possible. The whole Division bids him God-speed, and our congratulations and good wishes are none the less hearty if with them are mixed the natural regrets one feels at losing a good pal. We cannot close without extending a hearty welcome to his successor.

Correspondence.

To the Editor,
  " B.E.F Times."

Sir,
  If you will kindly supply me with the name and address of your correspondent signing himself a " Lover of Nature," I will guarantee that he will not love Nature any more; neither will he hear any more cuckoos. No sir! not this Spring nor next or any other Spring neither. Cuckoo indeed!! I'll learn 'im.

Yours Faithfully,
  " FED UP "

Agony Column.

MINNIE.—Meet me at Flying Pig 8 30.—Tock Emma.

M O.—Young, inexperienced, would like appointment with fighting battalion to gain experience.—Write M.O.

FOR SALE or EXCHANGE.—Large Country ESTATE, pleasantly situated on the banks of the Somme. Owner travelling East for the benefit of his health. No reasonable offer refused, would exchange for a couple of white rabbits, or something edible.

MESSRS. ABDUL & CO. regret that, owing to unforseen troubles, they ARE UNABLE TO SUPPLY any more Turkish Delights for the present, as there has been such a run on them.

But I'm not King! no Bill, I'm not the King,
So 'spose I've got to hump the blasted thing,
Gawd 'elp the 'un I get my 'ands upon,
One moment 'ere, and passing thence, 'e's gone,
'Tis soon we'll 'ave the blighter on a string.
" Gawd save the King, yus Bill! Gawd save the King."

There was a little Turk, and Baghdad was his home,
There was a little Hun, and he lived in Bapaume,
Each said to the other, as they shivered with alarm,
" To find another home wouldn't do us any harm."

Publisher's Announcements.

MESSRS. STODGER AND STOUTUN.

GOD'S GOOD MAN—An Autobiography by William Hohenzollern (Author of "The Innocents' Abroad," "Misunderstood," "The Christian," etc.)

A THIEF IN THE NIGHT—By Little Willie.

THE LAST HOPE—Professor Hindenberg (Author of "Westward Ho.")

IT'S NEVER TOO LATE TO MEND—Dr. Wilson.

ERIC, OR LITTLE BY LITTLE—Dean Haig.

THE CRUISE OF THE CATCH-A-LOT— By Bill Beatty.

THE DRINK HABIT
ACQUIRED IN THREE DAYS.

If you know anyone who doesn't drink alcohol regularly, or occasionally, let me send my free book, "CONFESSIONS OF AN ALCOHOL SLAVE." It explains something important, i.e.: How to quickly become an

Expert "Bona-fide Toper."

For the first 15 years of my life I was a rabid teetotaler, since the age of 16 I have never been to bed sober. If your trouble is with reference to a friend please state in your letter whether he is willing to be cured or not. Letters treated in a confidental manner. I can cure anyone.

Address : J. SUPITUP, Havanotha Mansions.   Telegrams : " RATS."

THE FOSSILEUM

—o—o—o—o—

THE DUMA TROUPE OF QUICK CHANGE ARTISTS

STARRING :—

Rodzi & Co., in their Stirring Domestic Drama,

"SPRING CLEANING."

—o—o—o—o—

Great American Film Play, Entitled :--

"TEDDY GET YOUR GUN

(SOME FILM) FEATURING THEODORE IN THE LEAD.

—o—o—o—o—

Murray's Colourmatrograph.

A TOUR THROUGH PALESTINE (Series.
NO. 3: JERUSALEM.

EDITORIAL.

SPRING has at last really come! And with it an unusual amount of hurry and bustle all round ; likewise forecasts, prophecies and conjectures, all frothy and furious We have all put our watches on one hour, and are now spending our spare time throwing away our surplus kit, sharpening our pistols and swords. and having our boots soled and heeled. We are also trying to produce this number of the paper under rather more difficult circumstances than usual, and we feel sure that our gentle readers will understand that whatever may be lacking is due to circumstances over which we have no control. We have again been fortunate in obtaining a special article from the pencil, ink, copying, one, of our old friend Mr. Teech-

Bomas, which we feel sure will be read with interest. This number sees the finish of our serial "Narpoo Rum," and we wish to remind our readers of our Mammoth Competition in connection with same, particulars of which we published in our Grand Xmas Double Number last December. We still have several million francs left in our treasure chest which we should like to dispose of before the "Big Push" commences, more on account of its bulk than for any other reason. It may be a long time before we can produce another number, in which case we wish to take this opportunity of bidding all our friends "au revoir," the best of luck, and thanking them all for the kind support we have always received since the day in "Wipers" long ago when we found an old printing outfit looking for a job.

THE EDITOR.

NEWS FROM THE RATION DUMP.

—o—o—o—

The Esquimaux have broken off diplomatic relations with Germany.

—o—o—o—

The Huns are shortening their line in the West with a view to sending a number of divisions on a punitive expedition against them

—o—o—o—

Patrols of British and French cavalry swam the Rhine last night near Cologne, and are now meeting with sharp resistance in the suburbs of Berlin.

—o—o—o—

A party of A.S.C. were seen working in the reserve line.

—o—o—o—

The Czar of Russia has antiquated.

—o—o—o—

Horatio Bottomley has accepted the Turkish throne on condition they make a separate peace.

—o—o—o—

Leave is about to re-open on the Western front.

—o—o—o—

The German fleet has bombarded Wapping Old Stairs, and ruined the carpet.

—o—o—o—

40,000 Huns have surrendered. They were so thin that they walked down one of our C.T.'s in fours.

—o—o—o—

[The Editor takes no responsibility for the truth of the above statements.]

TEN GERMAN PIONEERS.

Ten German Pioneers went to lay a
    mine,
One dropped his cigarette, and then
    there were nine.

Nine German Pioneers singing Hymns
    of Hate,
One stopped a whizz-bang, and then
    there were eight.

Eight German Pioneers dreaming hard
    of Heaven,
One caught a Flying Pig, and then
    there were seven.

Seven German Pioneers working hard
    with picks,
One picked his neighbour off, and then
    there were six.

Six German Pioneers, glad to be alive,
One was sent to Verdun, and then there
    were five.

Five German Pioneers, didn't like the
    war,
One shouted " Kamarad," and then
    there were four.

Four German Pioneers tried to fell a
    tree,
One felled himself instead, and then
    there were three.

Three German Pioneers, prospects very
    blue,
One tried to stop a tank and then there
    were two.

Two German Pioneers walked into a
    gun,
The gunner pulled the lanyard, and then
    there was one.

One German Pioneer couldn't see the
    fun
Of being shot at any more, and so the
    war was done.

ON THE HEELS OF THE FLEEING FOE.

—o—o—o—

FROM TEECH BOMAS.

—o—o—

FRANCE, Sunday Afternoon.

This morning, many hours before dawn, I mounted my bicycle and rode through 174 of the 187 blasted villages liberated during the past couple of days by our troops. I am now in the 175th, 12 miles north-south-west of Peraume, seated in what remains of the bar parlour of its main Estaminet, eating a frugal meal, and talking to the oldest inhabitant. I have this moment tasted a mouthful of Hun ration bread, which the enemy was unable to destroy in his hurried departure. It is darkish blue-black in hue, and its taste is putrid, rancid, nauseating, foul and stinking.

The scenes I have personally witnessed to-day as I rapidly pedalled into village after village were thrilling, awe-inspiring, blood-curdling—in short the whole outfit was EPIC. Old men, young men, women, girls, cripples, hunchbacks, little children, large children, all in their gladdest clothes, cheered me to the echo as I flashed through the various villages, whilst the village bands played patriotic airs in the market places. Occasionally I dismounted and talked to the people. To one woman I said "What of the Hun officers?" She gave a low shrill whistle and replied with emotion "Bosch officier, no bon, plenty zig-zag." This incident, in itself trivial, sums up the situation.

On my way from the 174th to the 175th village I found myself in front of our own outposts, and amongst those of the enemy. Rapidly twisting up the ends of my moustache and turning my cap inside out, I was able to escape recognition, and observed the antics of the Hun rearguard from closer quarters than anyone has ever done before. Officers and men, Unteroffiziere, Feldwebel and Freijährige, were all gibbering with fright, and pale pink drops of sweat dripped and dropped from their mottled brows as they leapt from tree to tree.

Just before reaching this village, an exciting and almost touching incident occurred. A very tired German 17-inch shell came sizzling through the air, and burst right under my cycle. Luckily the only damage done was a slight puncture to my near off side wheel. This proves how the Bosch H E has deteriorated during the past few months.

Even now I can hear the battle raging in the near distance. I must away and leave to a later dispatch the narrative of what I shall do and see this afternoon.

ARMA VIRUMQUE CANO.

—o—o—o—

No Prayers of Peace for me; no maiden's
    sigh.
Give me the Chants of War, the Viking's
    Song;
Battle for me; nor care I for how long
This war goes on. Tell me, where
    bullets fly;
Where noble men and brave may bleed
    and die;
Where skilful parry foils the sword-thrust
    strong.
Such are the tales I love. (I may be
    wrong—
A warrior, and no carpet knight am I.)

—o—o—o—

The D.S.O., the M.C. grace my breast;
My brow is bound with laurels and with
    lace;
I love this war. Perhaps you think that
    that
Is strange. Well I am different from the
    rest
Of you poor blighters. I live at the Base,
And use the Brain inside my nice, red hat.

C. L. P.

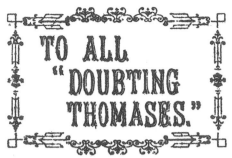

TO ALL "DOUBTING THOMASES."

Now listen ye of mournful mien, whose
bleatings rend the air,
Who spread an air of gloom where'er
you go,
That though of cleverness you have p'r'aps
more than your fair share,
Yet most of us just hate your wail of woe.
—o—o—o—
One day 'tis "this" and next day "that,"
your bogies come at will,
Of fearful ills to come you rave and rant,
You said a year ago the war was lost—
we're fighting still,
The job has been no easier for your cant.
—o—o—o—
In reverse you see disaster, and a victory
spurs you on
To still greater efforts in the realms of
doubt,
"We'll be lured into a trap," or "we
can ne'er hold what we've won,"
And "we'll all be starved to death" your
constant shout.
—o—o—o—
Tis true that mostly you are those who
ne'er have known the joy
Of living in ten feet of mud and slime,
Or the ecstasy which thrills one, sheer
delight without alloy,
When you're dodging crumps and
Minnies all the time.
—o—o—o—
So in future cut the grousing, and for
God's sake wear a grin,
The time is surely coming in a while,
When in spite of all your croakings the
old Huns will be "all in,"
Cut the everlasting wail and smile, man,
SMILE !

CONCERNING APOLOGIES.

A RHYME NOT WITHOUT REASON.

"Only the Wise apologise,
Fools always must explain."
(Extract from a Great
Modern Poet.)
—o—o—o—
On receipt of our verses, the Gunner
grew pensive,
But quickly developed a counter-offensive;
And though the rounds mostly were
duds, or fell short,
They showed themselves able to make
some retort.
—o—o—o—
We all know the Sappers, of course,
never shirk
From anything looking the least bit like
WORK ;
So pale, but determined, they swore,
"He shall rue it ! "
And asked for two large Working Parties
to do it.
—o—o—o—
The Staff, though surprised, did not
gibber or storm,
But dealt with it all on the Authorised
Form ;
For "G" said, "Well, I know whom
THAT refers to,"
And passed the whole matter "for
action" to "Q";
While "Q" patronisingly gave it a
smile,
Remarked, "Poor old 'G' Branch ! "
and wrote on it "FILE."

P.B.I

A STORY WITHOUT A MORAL.

—o—o—o—

And it came to pass that upon a certain day the General Officer Commanding a Division said unto his A.A and Q.M.G.: " O A.A. and Q.M.G., tender unto me by the first day of next month a Return showing the names of the number of men of this Division who have even refused to undergo the hardships of INOCULATION, in order that I may send forward this Return unto Corps., in accordance with C R.O. 758

And it came to pass that the A.A. and Q.M.G. said certain things unto his D.A.A. and Q.M.G. and unto his D.A.Q.M.G., the result of which was a Return of names to the number of fifty of men of the Division who had refused to be INOCULATED.

And it came to pass that the Return aforementioned was in due course sent forward unto Corps., in which place it became labelled with the mystic sign " P.A.," which, being interpreted, means " put aside."

And it came to pass that upon a much later date this same General Officer Commanding a Division said unto his A.A. and Q.M.G.: " O A.A. and Q.M.G. render unto me by the first day of next month a Return showing the names of the number of men of this Division who have done deeds such as are worthy of reward in the form of the Medal Military, in order that I may send forward this return unto Corps., in accordance with C.R.O. 869.

And it came to pass that this Return also was duly obtained, and in due course sent forward unto Corps., in which place it became labelled with the mystic sign " P.A.," which, being interpreted, means " put aside."

And it came to pass that in due course those men who had refused to be INOCULATED were duly awarded with the MILITARY MEDAL.

Oh ! great is the Corps.

Verbatim Extracts From Intelligence Summaries.

—o—o—o—

TRENCH MORTARS.

—o—

At 1·0 p.m. the " Flying Pig " dropped a round in our front line at X 9 d 5 2. The trench was completely wrecked—the crater formed being 14 feet deep and 25 feet across It is consoling to think that over 40 rounds have been fired from this gun into the enemy trenches during the last week.

(Very consoling to the P.B.I.)

—o—o—o—

OPERATIONS.

—o—

On the 21st, in W 6 b, a party of about 10 Germans entered our lines. Our bombers, however, drove them out, in addition to killing 5 of them.

(SOME bombers !)

—o—o—o—

MOVEMENTS.

—o—

At Z 5 b 21 this morning about thirty men were seen doing Expended Order Drill.

(We hope it wasn't painful.)

The following is a true extract from a return of reserve rations from a certain garrison :—

Locality—Foxhall Keep.
Map Ref.—P 67 X 19-32.
Commodity—Bully Beef.
Quantity—1 Tin.
Remarks—Not Full.

(Where's Lord DEVONPORT ?)

Rubályát of William Hohenzollern.

Awake, old Tirpz! Bid Hindenburg
arise,
" Der Tag " has come, I long to hear
the cries
Of Europe! We'll proceed to raise all
Hell,
Let's use our day from dawn. Time
flies! Time flies!

—o—o—o—

Dreaming, it seemed to me the World
was mine,
Waking, I think that the idea is fine ;
We'll wade right in to see what we can
grab,
And glut ourselves with murder, rape
and wine.

—o—o—o—

Come, fill the cup, and don a mask of
pain
That we should have to cleanse the
World again ;
Consider we our cause both pure and
strong,
So first we'll try our hand in old Louvain.

—o—o—o—

Should any doubt my will, or us dispute,
Man, woman, child, don't hesitate to
shoot ;
We'll play the policeman, and for
Kultur's sake
My son, young Bill, will pick up all the
loot.

—o—o—o—

How sweet is mortal sov'reignty—you
see
How sov'reignty has made a God of me,
As I a God of it—play we the role
Thus, each one part, and that alternately.

I sometimes think that never lived so
great
A monarch as myself—in fact of late
My greatness has appalled me and I
bow,
I bow my humbled head upon the gate

—o—o—o—

There is no door, but that we have the
key,
There is no depth debarred from you
and me,
Success alone will justify our game,
So kill the land and terrorise the sea.

—o—o—o—

And if the man you burn, the child you
kill,
Should even for one moment keep you
still,
Think well 'tis for our sacred Kultur's
sake,
And by a million murders steel your
will.

—o— o—o—

Yet should success to dust and ashes
fade,
And Justice rise from out the Hell we
made,
We'll say that others lit the fire, and we
But fanned the flames, to mark the price
they paid.

—o—o—o—

So Tirpz! with Hindenburg and me
conspire,
With murder, rapine, frightfulness and
fire,
Let's raise all Hell and, even should we
fail,
At least we'll have " Der Tag " of our
desire.

HOW CONGRESS DECLARED WAR.

—o—o—o—

BY

OUR SPECIAL CORRESPONDENT

Tuckis Shurtin.

—o—o—o—

MR. TUCKIS SHURTIN managed, by the wonderful enterprise and skill always shown by him on these delicate operations, to hide himself behind a life-size picture of Charlie Chaplin in the White House, and was thus present at the most momentous meeting which ever took place in the history of America.

He briefly describes, in his own picturesque language, exactly what took place.

" Wal ! " said Woodrow, chewing the end of a five-cent che-root, " I'm for a show-down."

The Bull-Moose took the floor and bucked, good and plenty. " Say," he howls, " double the ante, and raise 'em sky-high for cards. I ain't in on a two-dime game. Cut it out. I'm in on a no limit, and I've got the dust. Give me half a-million boys, and I'll skin every Hun in Yurrup. Yes ! sirree ! !

Elihu P. showed a busted straight, and beat for the golden silence.

Big Bill threw in for the Bull-Moose, leaving Woodrow up against it.

" Wal ! " said he, " write me down for a two-cent boob if I don't hand it to Willie. Say, boys, I'm in the game. Boost the ante, and sky-high for cards. I'm a bold she-wolf, and it's my night to howl."

" Rah ! RAH ! RAH ! Woodrow. Oh ! Willie, beat it ! Theo's on your track, and he's hungry.

TUCKIS SHURTIN.

THEY DIDN'T BELIEVE ME !

—o—

Don't know how it happened quite,
Sure the jar came up all right ?
Just as full as it should be
Wouldn't touch it, no, not me !
Sergeants very seldom touch
Rum, at least, not very much,
Must have been the A.S.C..
Anyway, it wasn't me !

Yet when I told them that I hadn't
touched the jar,
They didn't believe me, they didn't
believe me ;
They seem to know a sergeant's thirst,
I fear they all believe the worst,
It's the rottenest luck that there could
be ;
And when I tell them, and I'm certainly
going to tell them,
There'll be fatigues for them where'er I
be,
They'll never believe me, they'll never
believe that
The man who tapped the jar could not
be me !

Stop Press News.

Rioting is again reported in Berlin. The Kaiser has gone to bed with whooping cough and ricketts.

—o—o—o—

The New German War Loan has reached the stupendous figure of 50,000 marks owing to the successful U Boat campaign.

—o—o—o—

Two juvenile food hogs were arrested yesterday. On examination it was found that their pockets were full of brandy balls.

"AU REVOIR."

—:o:—

" 'Tis sad but true," that with nearly every issue of the paper we have to reserve this column in order to say good-bye to some distinguished member of the Division.

This time it is our late C R.E , Brig.-General A. Craven.

We wish to offer him our most hearty congratulations on his hard earned and well-deserved promotion, and, at the same time, say how much we shall all miss him.

He has always been a very good friend to us all, and a staunch supporter of the paper, and we should like him to know how much the whole Division appreciates his ever ready assistance, and the considerations he has always shown both in work and play.

Good luck and God speed.

Don't sit up for the mine, Daddy ! don't sit up for the mine !
Let's go to our Chateau at Walton Heath, and to bed at half-past nine,
Mary can call us for zero hour, if she wakes us about 3·9,
We'll hear the big bang at 3·10, you see, so don't sit up for the mine.

Correspondence.

To the Editor,
" B.E.F. Times."

Sir,

Once again I feel constrained to draw your attention to the increasing rowdiness of the district. I am a peaceful citizen, and although somewhat behindhand with my rates, yet the injustice of the present conditions is apparent. Surely, when a quiet citizen wishes to cultivate his own small holding, it is not quite the thing to plant a 12-inch howitzer in the middle. I must protest, and if nothing is done in the matter, I announce my intention of voting against the present candidate at the forthcoming election.

I am, Sir,
FED-UP.

Our Short Story.

—o—o—o—

There once was a teetotal Q.M.
* * * * * * *

THE END.

SONG OF ANY INFANTRY BRIGADIER TO HIS MEN.

In my dug-out (where the plans are laid)
I sing this song to my Brigade.
You chaps who in a scrap have been
Will " compris " fully what I mean.
Just lately in the stunts you've struck,
You haven't had the best of luck.
You've had the kicks without the pence,
And always struck a stiffish fence.
You've had the mud: you've had the wet:
You've had the shells as well.   And yet
You never grumble—just hold on
When all except your pluck has gone.
We know the cheery way you curse
When things are getting worse and
                worse,
Yet if I ask for further work,
There's not a dammed one here would
                shirk ;
The Higher Staff quite understand,
But know the old Division, and
They know that they have but to ask,
And you will carry out the task.
So I have pledged my knightly word
To stick it out until the Third.
And though I pledge it with remorse
I pledge it hopefully ; because
I know the stuff of which you're made,
I know the old " Umpteenth " Brigade.
I know you'll always play the game
(Although it is a b * * * * y shame),
And so in tempest and in rain,
In shells and shells, and shells again,
Just understand (it's nothing new ?)
How proud I am of all of you.

TO THE MEMORY OF

Lt.-Col. E. R. MOBBS, D.S O.

Lt.-Col. H. W. COMPTON.

Lt.-Col. H.V.M. DE LA FONTAINE,
                D.S.O.,

and those others who have left

us lately.

Two swift hours in a Pullman car
Aboard and afloat, and you're back again
In the land of the crump and the shooting
                star,
And you fight for a place in the old Pop.
                train,
Fifteen hours—rather more than less—
Of discomfort and boredom, and then
                you reach
(If you're lucky) your railhead, and then
                you guess
That some of the bloom is off the peach
                Of ten days leave.

WE ATTACK AT DAWN.

—:o:—

BY OUR SPECIAL CORRESPONDENT
Mr. Teech Bomas.

—:o:—

All was still as the first flush of dawn lit the sky. Then suddenly the atmosphere was riven by the crescendo chorus which leapt to meet the light as a bridegroom to his bride. The delicate mauve and claret of the dawning day was displaced by a frothy, and furious fandango of fire. The giant trogolythic ichnyosaurus crept fawning from their lairs, and gambolled their way to the line oblivions of anything that barred their passage. The disgruntled bosom of mother earth heaved with spasmodic writhings as the terrible tornado tore the trees. I was picking wallflowers in Glencorse Wood when all this happened, and even now the memory of that zero hour is with me. Having passed through several liberated villages, I stood on that historic spot and waited to put my watch right by the barrage. It came, and the world wilted. Then on came the gallant Esquimaux and Peruvians (I musn't mention anything English, it isn't "done,") and with a wild rush shattered Germany's grey-clad hosts. The while the guns thundered and boomed in hellish chorus across the riven bosom of Belgium, the wild flowers grew and the birds sang, revelling in hectic competition with their human rivals who figured in fantastic feats turning many a lark green with envy. Even the tanks, catching the atmosphere of excitement, threw cartwheels in an earnest endeavour to camouflage their real nature. Many parties of Huns were so surprised at their appearance that they offered them bird seed. In fact we attacked at dawn.

TEECH BOMAS.

ROADS.

Belgium, rain, and a sea of mud,
The first seven years are, they say, the worst ;
The pavé roads when you're spitting blood,
And all you have is a priceless thirst.

—o—o—o—

From Café Belge down to Kruistraathoek
In the same old rain, and the same old din ;
From Hell-fire Corner to Bellewarde Brook,
With the transport rattling on like sin.

—o—o—o—

We trod those roads in the days gone by
'Till we knew each brick, or shell-struck tree ;
When the war was young, and our hopes ran high
That the summer would give us the victory.

—o—o—o—

Staggered along in the same old slush,
Dodging the crump-holes where one could ;
Cursing all night, 'till the new-dawn's blush
Found us just flitting from Zouave Wood.

—o—o—o—

Much has been changed, but never the roads,
Each may be different yet each the same;
The same dammed pavé, the same dammed loads,
And fewer return by the road we came.

—o—o—o—

Maybe one day we'll forget the rain,
The mud and the filth of a Belgian scene;
But always in mem'ry I'll see again
Those roads with the stumps where the trees had been.

GREAT LABOUR MEETING AT DICKEBUSH.

—:o:—

Flamsey MacBonald in the Chair.

—:o:—

Last night, Flamsey MacBonald addressed a large and sympathetic audience at the Town Hall, Dickebush. Powerful support was given by Messrs. Grictor Vayson, A. Tenderson and a host of other hard (working) labourites. Mr. Mac Bonald commenced by saying that the war should be stopped (loud and unanimous cheering,) and said that if they only sent him to Christiania he would see to it. (A heckler here suggested that sending him to hell might help matters.) He said that he had the interests of the working man at heart. (Loud and unanimous cheers from Grictor Vayson.) When asked "Who the devil asked you to look after the working man, why not get on with a job yourself." Mr Flamsey only looked pained and surprised at the ingratitude of the working man who grudged him his self-appointed task of doing nothing at four hundred pounds a year. However, strong and vigorous speeches, which cut the usual amount of ice, followed in rapid succession from these eminent labourites. Mr. Grictor Vayson was just getting well away when a whizz bang fell within a couple of miles. As all present had every desire to avoid any harm happening to these modest delegates, a rush was made to the platform to safeguard them from danger. They, however, had already left, so that the citizens of Dickebush were prevented from wishing them God-speed.

BOIS DE RIAUMONT STAKES.

—:o:—

We have pleasure in recording the result of this classic event, which took place over the well-known course under rather trying conditions, in the spring of this year. At the same time we must apologise for its somewhat tardy appearance in print. The ante-post betting rather favoured "The Professor," but "Reggie" was heavily supported at about a point more, and there was quite a lot of money for "Bill Buggan." This latter is a good looker but with—at this time— no public performances to his credit in this part of the world so the public were naturally shy about putting too much faith in the training reports. Punctually on schedule time the gate went up, and a magnificent start was witnessed. The three favourites got away in a bunch with a little fancied starter called "Sapper." The going was bad, but the pace was good, and it was anyone's race at the distance. "Reggie," however, here made a strong bid and came to the front, and although strongly challenged by "The Professor," won a good race by a neck. A length away came "Bill Buggan" going well, with "Sapper" fourth. They were greeted with loud cheers from their backers, but a prolonged fusilade of groans from the Hun bookmakers who had evidently lost a large packet on the event.

ROBIN HOODFELLOW.

One named Kaiser Bill, thought the
    world he could fill
With Kultur of his special making,
But after three years finds himself full of
    fears
For himself and his throne that is
    shaking.

A POPULAR B.T.O. TO HIS MOUSTACHE.

—o—o—o—

Now, you are gone, I did not know
before,

How I should miss you, when you came
to pass.

Together, we have quaffed the Bottled
Bass,

The Whiskey Cup, the Ale=for half a
score

Of happy years, or haply even more.

And oft together, from a single glass,

The Wine of Life we sipped ; but now,
alas,

For you, no more, this vintage, stewards
pour.

—o—o—o—

Often, I touched, with trembling finger
tips,

Your treasured form, your pulchritude.
that lay

Quiescent, silent, beauteous, night and
day ;

Or felt your fragrance pressed upon my
lips.

But five short minutes in the barber's
chair,

And you were gone—my upper lip is bare.

C.L.P.

When the golden sun sets in the West,
And the sausages all go to roost,
   Tho' the rain may be o'er,
   We shall soon have some more,
And the Hun comes with bombs us to
boost,
When the Archies should all be in bed,
They are kicking up Hell with a zest,
   And the noise of the day,
   Hasn't all passed away,
From my camouflaged tent in the West.

ARMY TERMS AND THEIR DERIVATION.

—o—o—o—

G O:C.—Gold or carrots. Owes its origin to the gaudy colours affected.

—§ † §—

CAMOUFLAGE —From camel and flag, referring to the device adopted by this animal of tying a flag to its tail, and thus disguising itself as a ship of the desert. Hence—to deceive.

—§ † §—

A.P.M.—Awfully polite men. Originated in the politeness with which these people bandy airy persiflage with Transport Officers.

—§ † §—

T.O.—Ticked oft. (See A.P.M.)

—§ † §—

M.L.O.—Medals and leave often. Reason obscure.

—§ † §—

TRENCH.—So called from the trenchant remarks from those inhabiting them.

—§ † §—

AREA COMMANDANT.—See dug out.

—§ † §—

ARCHIE.—So called after William Tell who shot so dexterously that he split the apple.

—§ † §—

DUG-OUT.—Of two kinds. The name originates in a habit of the early natives who excavated holes for themselves to avoid the slings and arrows of the enemy. Another kind is the erection in which Area Commandants dwell.

OUR SALE OR EXCHANGE COLUMN.

—:o:—

This branch has been established for the convenience of our subscribers and all small wants are advertised at a reasonable charge.

—o—o—o—

WANTED.—To rent for the winter season, DRY WARM DUG OUT. Must be commodious and in healthy locality ; untroubled by hawkers and Huns. Good price offered for suitable residence. Apply.—Reggie, c/o of this paper.

FOR SALE.—TWO TANKS. Slightly soiled. Price moderate. Or would exchange for a pair of rabbits Apply.— 41, Dammstrasse.

FOR SALE.—PLEASANT COUNTY ESTATE, situated in one of the nicest parts of Belgium. Heavily wooded. Has been shot over. Owner desirous of leaving. Apply. Feddup, Glencorse Wood.

FOR EXCHANGE.—TWO FIELD DRESSINGS, in good condition, and ONE IODINE AMPOULE (unused.) Would exchange for HATBAND and TABS (red or blue—the latter preferred.) Write.— Harassed, Canada Street.

GENTLEMAN, Young, in sixth form at Oxford and Cambridge Colleges, feels that his talents are wasted in the P.B.I. Would like a job cleaning the windows of a leave boat. Apply.—One Pip, Krab Krawl.

SEVERAL YOUNG GENTLEMEN, with University degrees (Heidelburg) would like to be taken as boarders in English country districts. Would do agriculture labour in exchange for lodging and keep. Apply—Fritz, Lens.

CRICKET.

—o—o—o—

BY OUR SPECIAL CORRESPONDENT

MR. F. B. PILSEN.

—o—

The pitch was the real thing for the spheriod when the Hoppers took the field. Old Sol was not in a kindly mood, but otherwise it was a good day for the King of Sports. The lads from the Midlands took first knock, and two of their stalwarts marched out into the arena to do battle with the champions of the Hop County. The latter's trundler got off the mark well, and a well-placed effort soon beat the guardians of the ash grove and shattered Number One's timber yard—one for three. The wielders of the willow were unable to get hold of the leather, and only notched 23 all told, Mr. Extras being responsible for the majority

Then it was the turn of the lads from Kent. Their skipper didn't cause the gentleman with the pad and pencil to develop writer's cramp, as he misjudged a cunningly delivered sphere from the opposing O.C , which spread-eagled his pegs. After this however, despite some good mixing by the lanky American expert, they managed to collect a good enough bunch, and the Notts and Jocks had a merry time chasing the elusive pillule. The tail wagged feebly however, and in the end the lads from the Strawberry County only clicked by three chips.

THROUGH PRUSSIAN PINCE-NEZ.

—o—o—o—

We reproduce below a few extracts from the Prussian papers which have fallen into our hands lately. They all tend to show the wilful misrepresentation of facts which is rife in the German Press.

The following is a free translation of an article in "Wurst und Sauerkraut," a leading Berlin daily :—"We have it on the best authority that the English are on their last legs. Our secret agents report that in many places the people are getting so thin that gratings in the streets are being carefully fenced off. Also that the Ladies' Grill in the House of Parliament is being closed, as this famous restaurant is so short of the tasty chops and steaks which delighted the hearts of the female English."

Following from "Die Schweinhund" :—"Our London agent reports that the last reserves of man power have already been eaten up by our brave field greys, and that the English pigs are calling up children now. He yesterday saw one of eight years in the abominable khaki. What can our brave airmen have been doing?

Following from "Die Potsdammerung" :—"Herr Von Tirpitz yesterday made a glorious speech praising our brave sailors. Our gallant matlows sing twice daily the Hymn of Hate, and we are sorry for the English Fleet if they ever should dare to tackle our men. That, as Herr Von Tirpitz said, is not to be expected as the cowards stay outside, and nothing can tempt them up the Kiel Canal. However our noble-never-to-be-despised sailors will put up with the disappointment, and sing the Hymn three times daily in future."

Following from "Die Schnitzel" :—"The All High and Mightiest condescended to address his brave Pomeranians yesterday. He said : My brave-and-never-to-be-defeated-while · Wolff-and-I-are alive Pomeranians, once more you have a victory over the Pig-dog enemy gained. You waited till they nearly-up-to-you were, yet could they not catch you. I your War Lord say that you saviours of the Fatherland are. Your bread ration doubled-be-shall when our gallant U Boats bring us flour. Go now and beat the swine English again. I am your War Lord and the All Highest. Take my blessing and pull in your belts. I'm going to dine.' "

JE NE LE PENSE PAS.

Sing of the joys of a transport man,
Who drives along with a gay " Hallo ! "
Cracking his whip as he only can,
A smile and a joke as away they go.

—:o:—

His cap is jauntily placed on his head,
His clothes show the care of an old-time beau,
He hums to the tune that his mules' hooves tread,
His voice runs in dulcet tones and low.

—:o:—

With a load of duckboards he threads his way
Through the sylvan glades where the pavé runs.
And nothing can ruffle him night or day
As he brings up timber, or food for the guns.

—:o:—

Driving along on the smooth hard roads,
With never a jolt and never an oath,
Till at Hell Fire Corner he drops his loads,
And fondles his mules, for he loves them both.

—:o:—

Then homeward he wends his weary way
To the rose-decked villa, where he may sleep
Till night shall again give place to day,
And the angels above him their vigil keep.

Correspondence.

To the Editor,
"B.E.F. Times."

Sir,

May I ask you to use your weight to obtain some special recognition for those, who like myself, enlisted almost at the outbreak of war, and have never yet been to the front line. Surely martyrs like ourselves who have had to put up with soft jobs in England or at the base in France deserve some special recognition to compensate for the weary months we have spent with yearning hearts while others had all the fun of the front line. It is only our deep sense of duty which has kept us from breaking our bonds and going up the line. Is it too much to expect that some permanent and distinguishing badge should be given us ?

Yours, faithfully,
"E. TERNAL LEDSWINGER."

—o—o—o—

To the Editor,
"B.E.F. Times."

Sir,

We request your assistance in bringing to the notice of the city-fathers the night noises which are going on in the district. As ratepayers we must protest against the increasing noisiness of a set of hooligans who operate chiefly during the night hours, and who seem to rely chiefly on fireworks to make a disturbance in an otherwise peaceful village. Surely householders should be granted some protection as the district is rapidly becoming uninhabitable owing to motor buses, etc., which pass in one unending stream day and night and the performances of the band of night hooligans.

Yours, faithfully.
"INDIGNANS."

LATE NEWS FROM THE RATION DUMP.

—o—o—o—

The Germans are short of shells.

—:o:—

The Pope is raising an army to come and stop the war.

—:o:—

We have the supremacy of the air— ESPECIALLY AT NIGHT.

—:o:—

The Germans have no guns.

—:o:—

We are going to dig-in, and wait till the Chinese are ready.

—:o:—

The Kaiser has been arrested by Hindenburg, and shot as a spy.

—:o:—

The Kiel Canal is closed to the public, as wheels are being put on the German Fleet to enable them to deal with the tanks. [This must be a canard, as no practical people would consider wheels necessary in Flanders.]

—:o:—

The Germans have no bombs.

ANSWERS TO CORRESPONDENTS.

Owing to lack of space, answers to our numberless correspondents are unavoidably held over.

EDITORIAL.

Oh, to be in Belgium,
Now that Winter's here!

BEFORE this appears in print it's more than likely that the weather will have gone round to May, but certainly at present it seems that Summer is a thing of the past. Anyway, Winter will certainly be with us before we've had time to dig up our thick underclothing from the spare kit dump, Winter! What memories that word conjures up. Brisk exhilarating walks over the snow-clad plains of Belgium. Oh, my sainted aunt! Most of our English contemporaries seem to fill their columns with reports of the doings of some people called Ramsay Macdonald, Grayson and others We should have thought that there would have been no difficulty in finding copy nowadays, and to chronicle the doings of a few nonentities seems to argue a lack of knowledge of what the people want to read about. However these penny dailies are generally very slow in feeling the public pulse. The whole B.E.F. will welcome with open arms the latest recruits to it's ranks in the shape of the W.A.A.C. The designers are to be congratulated on the attractive uniform, and the morale of the troops has gone up 100 per cent. (so has the candidature for a spell at the base.) We must again remind everyone that copy is necessary and ask them to send in.

THE EDITOR.

IF THE RAIN AND THE WAR LAST.

The Summer had been long and cold,
And Intha Pink was growing old,
He stroked his hoary snow-white beard,
And gazed with eyes now long since
    bleared,
He scanned the waters deep and still,
And muttered grimly " Swelp me, Bill,
Unless ' Aunt Sally ' heaves in sight,
We'll get no rations up to-night ! "

—o—o—o—

" She's late," he said in husky tones,
From near his feet came strangled moans,
He peered below into the gloom,
And for a sodden form made room,
'Twas Atkins of the P.B.I.,
Who brought the news that Hooge was
    dry,
And 'less they steered a half-square
    right,
They'd get no rations up that night.

—o—o—o—

At last " Aunt Sally " hove in sight,
Old Intha hailed her with delight,
The rations soon were stowed inside.
And Atkins went to act as guide,
They steamed along at full six knots,
They dodged the shells, ignored the
    shots ;
In fact the future seemed quite bright,
They'd get the rations there that night.

But stay, what means that sickening
    scrape,
That left them stranded and agape ?
" Her bottom's out ! " old Intha cried,
And with a tin of biscuits tried
To stem the stream that flowed between
Her riven planks, but soon 'twas seen
That nothing now could put her right,
They'd get no rations up to-night.

—o—o—o—

'Twas now all hands to save themselves
On biscuit tins with pick-axe helves,
They rowed away, yet paused to find
The reason of their fate unkind . . . .
The waters, tired of rising higher,
Uncovered the Cathedral spire !
Uncharted, it had caused their plight,
No rations reached the line that night.

JIM.

—:o:—

A hard little, scarred little terrier,
With a touch of the sheep-dog thrown
    in—
    A mongrel—no matter,
    There's no better ratter
In trenches or billet, than Jim.

—:o:—

A tough little, rough little beggar ;
And merry, the eyes of him.
    But no Tartar or Turk
    Can do dirtier work
With an enemy rat, than Jim.

—:o:—

And when the light's done, and night's
    falling,
And the shadows are darkling and dim,
    In my coat you will nuzzle
    Your little pink muzzle
And growl in your dreams, little Jim,

            R.M.O.

HOW THE MEN OF BLANKSHIRE BAFFLED THE BERLINERS.

—:o:—

BY OUR SPECIAL CORRESPONDENT
Mr. TEECH BOMAS.

—:o:—

If was indeed a stirring episode of war in all it's terror and magnitude of sound. I am allowed to chronicle the epic deeds of the men from Blankshire who met the Berliners and bilked them with bayonets. The scene of this historic encounter was—well I musn't tell you that. The terrific tornado had torn the trees (as described in my last) and the blighting blast had battered the bark, but nothing could daunt the men from Blankshire. On they came kicking footballs, and so completely puzzled the Potsdammers. With one last kick they were amongst them with the bayonet, and although the Berliners battled bravely for a while, they kameraded with the best. 600 burly Berliners was the bag, and filled to overflowing the already replete cages. Then the still of night fell on this homeric contest. The little field mice continued their interrupted life, the only evidence that remained of what had transpired being the trampled sward whose greenness was here and there besmirched with an ever crimsoning crimson, and the rotund bodies of Berliners who had been a bit slow in kamerading. The larks sang and the flowers burst into bloom as another episode ended. Yet not closed, as all these episodes are but one episode. and the baffled Berliners battling the Blankshires is but typical of the events which, strung together, make the big offensive.

TEECH BOMAS.

WHAT A HOPE !

—o—o—o—

From Captain Bingham Jones, M.C ,

To Colonel Spanker,

   Dear Siree,
I have the honour to request,
That you will do your very best,
To recommend, and strongly too,
This my appeal I put to you,
To ask the G.O.C. if he,
His heart will soften, just for me,
My plea is nothing very mighty,
For four long months I've not seen
     Blighty,
If he a little-leave will grant,
I'll go and see my wealthy aunt,
Who's lying on a bed of pain ;
And never will get up again,
At least the doctor's say that's so,
And so I think I ought to go,
For if I don't I'm on the rocks,
The same applies to Messrs. Cox,
I therefore hope he will not choose,
My application to refuse,
And incidently I'll add,
That when this " hoped-for" leave
    I've had,
My work will please the C.R.E.,
As well as charm the G.O.C.
I have the honour, sir, to be,
Your humble servant, O.C. " D."

The sausage was a high one,
The Hun began to shoot,
He sniped his best with 9·2,
And said, " Ach ! dies ist gut,"
The airmen saw the little game,
And swooped down on that Hun,
Now Fritz is where all Fritzes go,
But hasn't got a gun.

EXCELSIOR 1917.

The shades of night were falling fast,
When up the muddy C.T. passed
A youth who bore, though looking glum,
A mighty gallon jar of rum.
    Excelsior !

—§ † §—

" Try not to pass," the sergeant said,
" The blasted Hun might shoot you
    dead,
He's sniping near, he's shelling far,
Perhaps he'll hit that blooming jar !
    So leave it 'ere."

—§ † §—

The youth moved on, no word spoke he
He wallowed up that old C.T.,
His visage grim showed pale in light
Where star shells glimmered through
    the night.
    Excelsior !

—§ † §—

" Stay ! stay ! my lad," the corp'ril
    cried,
" Another who the Hun defied
He got a bullet through the ' tum,'
And broke his blooming jar of rum,
    So go no more."

—§ † §—

The youth's sad face showed grim and
    pale,
He struggled on into the gale,
Passed whizz-bangs urgent in their
    flight
Where bullets pinged through deepest
    night,
    And rain did pour.

" 'Ere ! Alfred, stop ! " the private hailed,
The sad youth's face but paled and paled,
" Don't try that trench, the bloomin' 'un
Is sweeping it with many a gun,
    'E'll 'it the jar."

—§ † §—

" Ah ! stay me not," the youth replied,
" I must get there whate'er betide,
Though Hell may storm both near and
    far
I'll get there with this needed jar."
    He strode some more.

—§ † §—

At last his goal appears in sight,
And blatant minnies rack the night,
He staggers to the Coy. H.Q.,
And to the precious jar he's true—
    He still it bore.

—§ † §—

" Oh 'ell ! " the sergeant raging stormed,
Then to the job in hand he warmed,
He told that youth who proudly bore
The jar through all ! He told him more
    And more and more.

—§ † §—

He told him all about his past,
His future, present, and at last
He paused for breath, he gasped and
    died,
And dying fell he down beside
    An empty jar.

IT is with the greatest regret that we have to say "Good-bye" to one of the few remaining original members of the Division
    This loss will be deeply felt by those who have served with him for so long a time, and who have known that his never-failing kindness and support were available at any moment. We wish him " Good Luck " wherever he may go, and ask him to accept our gratitude for the help and encouragement he has given us in many difficult moments.

OUR DIARY.

—o—o—o—

BY LIEUT. SAMUEL PEPYS.

TO-DAY, at 4 of the clock, we did arrive at our new billets, feeling very fatigued and with a touch of the megrims. When we had inspected our billets we had a lot more of the megrims. One tells us that the Huns have a practice of shooting in the surroundings, so that we are all of a windiness. Orders have come, so it is said, that we shall depart from here very soon and go down to the activities. We have all got the megrims. To-day, at 5 of the clock, I saw her Ladyship of Dickebush in the Park, and was much struck by her appearance. Woodbines are up one penny on the packet, which does perturb us. ere is also a rumour that the R.T.O. of Bath has not got a decoration in the new list. This is not understandable, and savours of a canard. The morrow a small party of us must take the coach at the toll gate at P 21 C 2·4, and go to reconnoitre the field of battle. This is a most unlikeable business, and I have the megrims worse, so that the leech has given me a potion. Sardines are up two pennies the tin, which is a scandal, it occurs to me that there may be much profits accruing to some persons. Anne has writ to say that the enemy has appeared in some balloon or ship which flies, and has thrown exploding missiles at London. This has disturbed me much, as the taxes will not allow of the provision of new clothes for Anne if she should spoil her present ones. There is a story that no rum issue will be made this night. We all have the megrims, and whisky is up 2 francs on the bottle. This is a terrible war. I must be astir betimes in the morning with my new gas-bag. It is of a poor pattern, and I am very envious of that of Captain Spanker, whose is of a better quality. As to-morrow is also bath parade, to bed at 9 of the clock, tired and with the megrims.

A few more Military Terms Defined.

—o—o—o—

R.T.O.—Rude to officers. A pleasing brusqueness marks their manner when dealing with officers who have the impertinence to come away from the line for a spot of leave. This is affected to emphasise the strain of their position.

—:o:—

E.F.C.—Every franc counts. Derived from the thrifty methods of those A men employed therein, who evidently think that miss not, want not—after the war.

—:o:—

DUDS.—These are of two kinds. A shell on impact failing to explode is called a dud. They are unhappily not as plentiful as the other kind, which often draws a big salary and explodes for no reason. These are plentiful away from the fighting area.

WITH APOLOGIES TO RUDYARD KIPLING.

—o—o—o—

When you're waiting for zero, to go o'er
the top,
And yer mind gets a-wondering what
you will stop,
Just go to yer bottle, and neck a wee drop,
Cos thinkin' ain't good for a soldier.

—:o:—

When the 'un starts a barrage and you've
nowhere to go,
Don't wander round looking for dugouts
and so,
Just flop where you happen to be, don't
you know
Any 'ole's good enough for a soldier.

—:o:—

When yer click for a leave, and yer
warrant's come through,
Don't waste any time thinking what you
will do,
Just grab up yer pack, leg it quick fer
Berloo.
Any leave's good enough for a soldier.

TO A MARRAINE.

—o—o—o—

We are two bubbles in a glass of wine,
Smiling to one another, I and you,
Across the rosy sea, as if we knew,
That we should meet, some day, perhaps
to dine
Together, at some Bacchanalian shrine.
Chamelion-like, the wine takes on a hue
More roseate ; it smiles upon us two
In sympathy with this desire of mine.

—o—o—o—

We are two bubbles, floating in Life's
glass,
Transparent, joyous, fragile, delicate,
Pulsing with life and hope, to-day, we
seem ;
And yet, to-morrow, it may come to pass,
That some unshaven, cruel lip of Fate
May burst this fairy bubble of my dream.

C.L.P.

AS OF OLD.

—o—o—o—

It came to pass in the year one
thousand nine hundred and seventeen
that DAVID, a captain of the Hittiteshire
Regiment, did obtain a yellow parchment.
And with this parchment he did cross
the waters to the land of Berlighty, And
during his sojourn in this land he did
observe a woman bathing in the sea. And
he found her exceedingly beautiful to
gaze upon, so that he did ask of one
" Who is this lady ? " And they replied,
" She is the wife of one Lieut. URIAH, of
the Hittiteshires " And he did covet her
so much that he despatched a messenger,
even the buttons of her hotel, to her
apartments, bearing his greetings and
asking that she should break bread with
him. Which she did. And it came to
pass that the woman would not list to
his pleading. Thereon he became exceeding wroth, until on the eleventh day he
recrossed the waters and returned unto
his men. And it came to pass even as
he had wished that Lieut. URIAH was
sent unto him to be an officer under him.
Then became the heart of DAVID the
captain glad. And it came to pass that
certain elders became perturbed regarding
a citadel in the land of Noman, and
ordered the capture thereof. And even
as DAVID the captain and URIAH his
lieutenant were partaking of a mess of
Makonokie and Rhum came a messenger
bearing the tidings and instructions.
And lo ! the heart of DAVID was glad
Then said he unto the lieutenant " Thou
shalt take the forefront of the battle with
thy platoon. Haste or the judgment of
the Warofis will be upon thee." And
URIAH did fill himself with Rhum, and
likewise his platoon, and did sally forth.
Then did the heavens awake, and the
Amalekites did rage furiously having
much wind, and with slings and outrageous weapons did hurl vigorously
around. And it came to pass that DAVID,
the captain, was standing at the door of
his dug-out and did get a vertical gust.
And the enemy did hurl a wizbhang with
great violence, and did strike him on the
nose, and he did die of it. So it came
to pass that URIAH, the lieutenant, did
return, having captured the citadel, and
did find his captain dead. And he did
become captain in his stead.

MORAL.—A sub. in a dug-out's
worth two on the wire.

THE P.B.

I'm a twenty-one years soldier, and I
    want to tell no lies,
But the job I'm now engaged on feeds
    me right up to the eyes.

—§ † §—

Before the war in days of old, I ran a
    little show
Hawkin' rags and bones at Wigan, why
    I left it I don't know.

—§ † §—

But I heard the bugles callin', and join
    up I felt I must,
Now I wish I'd let them bugles go on
    blowin' till they bust.

—§ † §—

I joined to fight the Germans, and I
    crossed the angry sea.
Now I pick up bits of paper in a Depot,
    marked " P.B."

—§ † §—

It's a bloomin' waste of money sendin'
    me across the foam
To pick up bits of paper, I could do that
    job at home.

—§ † §—

And the soldiers. think it funny, that's
    what fills my bitter cup,
For they chuck down bits of paper just
    to see me pick 'em up.

—§ † §—

They keep me in the Depot, 'cause I've
    got a nasty wheeze,
D.A.H., and bad bronchitis, and I'm
    groggy at the knees.

I tried to get some leave I did, I said
    my wife was dead,
They found I'd never had a wife, and I
    got crimed instead.

—§ † §—

I tried to go to Orsepital, I showed a
    wobbly knee,
I got what I expected, number 9, and
    M and D.

—§ † §—

Last week they had a paper-chase, and
    all the Depots went ;
I had to follow up the 'ounds, and gather
    up the scent.

—§ † §—

On windy days they form a ring, and
    make a horse of me,
And back their bits of paper, ten to one
    against P.B.

—§ † §—

Once by mistake I found myself included
    in a draft,
The things that happened in the line
    have fairly turned me daft.

—§ † §—

I joined a working party going on up to
    the line,
The Hun he started shelling, so I thought
    I'd do a shine.

—§ † §—

I crawled into a drain-pipe to hide me
    from the Hun :
Then someone cried " Get out you fool,
    you're in a twelve-inch gun ! "

—§ † §—

I got back home—I don't know how—
    and saw the Batt. M.O.,
He passed me back again P.B., to where
    the sea winds blow.

—§ † §—

So here I am and here I'll stop ;. I'm
    bound to see it through,
I'll pick up bits of paper if my
    Country wants me to.
                H. H. W.

SEEN FROM AN AID-POST.

There are many roads in Flanders, where
the horses slide and fall,
There are roads of mud and pavé, that
lead nowhere at all,
They are roads, that finish at our trench;
the Germans hold the rest.
But of all the roads in Flanders, there is
one, I know the best.
It's a great road, a straight road, a road
that runs between
Two rows of broken poplars, that were
young and strong and green.

—o—o—o—

You can trace it from old Poperinghe,
through Vlamertinghe and Wipers ;
(It's a focus for Hun whiz-bangs and a
paradise for snipers)
Pass the solid Ramparts, and the
muddy moat you're then in,
The road I want to sing about—the road,
that leads to Menin.
It's a great road, a straight road, a road
that runs between
Two rows of broken poplars, that were
young and strong and green.

—o—o—o—

It's a road, that's cursed by smokers; for
you dare not show a light ;
It's a road, that's shunned by daytime ;
and is mainly used by night,
But at dusk the silent troops come up,
and limbers bring their loads
Of ammunition to the guns, that guard
the Salient's roads.
It's a great road, a straight road, a road
that runs between
Two rows of broken poplars, that were
young and strong and green.

And for hours and days together, I have
listened to the sound
Of German shrapnel overhead, while I
was underground
In a damp and cheerless cellar, continually
trying
To dress the wounded warriors, while
comforting the dying
On that muddy road, that bloody road,
that road that runs between
Two rows of broken poplars, that were
young and strong and green.

R.M.O.

A POET'S DEDICATION.

—o—o—o—

'Tis you, that are the fount of Inspiration,
Creator of my verses, sonnets, songs ;
To you, all credit for these lines,
belongs,
So, at your Shrine, I offer adoration
And dedicate to you this invocation.
For you, one wet and war-worn warrior
longs,
Forgetful of all daily cares and wrongs,
In the delight of nightly expectation.

—o—o—o—

O Motive Force, that makes a soldier
move
Great mountains of oppression from his
soul ;
Let others sing about the varied goal
Of Great Ambition, Women, War and
Love,
Such plaudits always leave me cold and
dumb,
Only your charms, I praise, O Tot o
Rum.

C.L.P.

SOMEWHERE IN—WIPERS.

—o—o—o—

By COCKLES TUMLEY.

—o—o—

(Our representative, Mr. COCKLES TUMLEY, has just paid a visit to the Front, and here describes his experiences in his inimitable manner.)

—o—

YOU can't imagine what I've seen. Neither can I! Stay, I will tell you.

I've worn a tin hat!

I've eaten a tin of bully beef!

I've talked with a general!

I won't tell you what he said, but you can take it from me THE WAR IS OVER.

I've been in the support line, which is much more dangerous than the first.

I've been in the reserve line, which is much more dangerous than the support.

I have been in Div. H.Q., which is more dangerous still.

And I have even been back to G.H.Q.

I have discussed the situation with the soldiers themselves. I can't tell you what they thought of it.

AND NOW FOR WHAT I HAVE LEARNT.

I have learnt that there's a lot of meat in a tin of bully. I have learnt that an army biscuit is a hard nut to crack. I have learnt that a tipping duckboard needs no push. I have learnt that Belgian beer wants a good deal of bush.

Every German prisoner I spoke to said the same thing. I can't tell you what it was, but THE WAR IS WON. To use one of our familiar slogans, I say "Watch the Q.M." I was having a talk with one of the Tommies who had answered the call of King and Country, and I asked him what he thought of it all. I can't tell you his answer, but it impressed me wonderfully. Well, I will write more next week when my head is clearer. I must go now and have my photo taken in a gas-bag and tin hat.

COCKLES TUMLEY.

AUNT ANNIE'S CORNER.

—o—o—o—

TENDER TALKS TO TINY TOTS.

—o—

MY Dear Little Tot-ties,

How have you been en-joy-ing your-selves all this time? Aunt Annie is very cross with you, as you have not written to her late-ly. This is very un-kind of you, as she brought you away from that nas-ty mud-dy place to the nice country. How-ever I know of the doings of some of you.

—:o:—

LIT TLE Billy Buggan has got a nice new house and a great big piece of land to play on, so he will be able to have great fun with his lit-tle friend Reg-gie.

—:o:—

TOMMY Flint went to a nice dog show the other day. He has moved into the coun-try and says that there are no naughty boys over the way to throw stones at him. He has got a lit-tle Scotch friend stay-ing with him.

—:o:—

PORKY and Jerry have been having a lot of games they tell me. I hope they have enjoyed themselves.

—:o:—

WE have got a lot of new Tot-ties who have joined our lit-tle cir-cle late-ly. They are all nice boys. I am sure we shall all be great friends, and play soldiers nicely together. Now that Xmas is coming we shall have a lot of parties. Won't that be nice Tot-ties? Lit-tle Jackie Shep-pard I think is going to give the first one.

—:o:—

Good-bye, Tot-ties,
Your Ev-er Lov-ing
AUNT ANNIE.

Correspondence.

To the Editor,
" B.E.F. Times."

Sir,

I shall be glad if you will spare a little space in your valuable paper to bring to the notice of your many readers the " Society for Providing Free Gin for Generals." This Society supplies a long felt want, and it's cause is entirely praiseworthy. " Jack " and " Tommy " have their rum provided by a benevolent government, what about our generals ? " Gin for Generals " should be on everyone's lips during the coming months. We are holding a soirée and sale of work next Saturday at the " Crab and Horseshoe " Hotel, where all are invited : some of the best people are giving their services. A collection will be made after the proceedings, and a small toll will also be levied for exit. I shall also be glad to receive subscriptions through the post.

Yours, etc.,

J. I. N. CRAWL,
Hon. Sec. S.P.F.G.G.

ANSWERS TO CORRESPONDENTS.

Owing to lack of space, answers to our numberless correspondents are still held over.

The Soldiers' Friend.

—o—o—o—

(With apologies to the " Daily Mail.")

—o—

MRS. P.—A soldier's pay ceases on the day on which he is killed.

—:o:—

WHISKY DISTILLER.—You should get total exemption, being engaged on work of national importance.

—:o:—

ANXIOUS WIFE. — Your separation allowance is probably correct. Your husband probably got a court-martial, and not a Field Marshal's job.

—:o:—

FLOSSIE.—Your husband had better consult his Regimental Medical Officer. He is sure to find him a very sympathetic person.

—:o:—

C 3.—As you say, total blindness should make you unfit for general service —appeal again.

—:o:—

" GUNNER."—No ; " Sage Femme " has two meanings.

ONCE again it is necessary to say " Good-bye " to our G.O.C. Short though the time was that was with us, yet in that time he had become popular with all ranks. We wish him the best of luck in the future. Also we take this opportunity of welcoming our new G.O.C , who will doubtless soon achieve the popularity enjoyed by his predecessors.

LITTLE WILLIE.—" When will our heaven-protected troops thrust back the hordes that seek to enter our sacred Vaterland, Papa ?"

BIG WILLIE.—
"When their Rawlies cease from Goughing,
And their Plumers Byng no more."

EDITORIAL.

FROM the look of things it doesn't seem that our paper will run many more numbers before we have the "Special Double Potsdam Number." We wonder how the Huns have managed to bribe Mr. Jupiter Pluvius, he is certainly the only one who has never failed them yet. We are reluctantly compelled to inform our subscribers that unless greater assistance is forthcoming in the shape of copy we shall be compelled to shut down. Eighteen months ago and even up to a year ago members of the Division used to help us by sending along copy, which always came in useful, although most sent a covering letter speaking rather modestly of their attached "efforts." But nowadays it is a very different story, and we think only two members of the Division make an attempt at helping us along. It cannot be lack of ability, so that we must put it down to either laziness or lack of interest, and, if the latter, then the sooner we shut down the better. We must say that we think greater enthusiasm might be shown in the sporting side of Divisional life, and that Div. football contests might be arranged more often. It generally follows that those who play well together work well together, and with the present scope it should be easy to arrange a cup or medal contest throughout the Division. Much could be done by the appointment of one committee member by Brigades, and the necessary arrangements can be made very easily. We will ask everyone in the Division to write something and send it along within the next fortnight, so that we may have a "Grand Xmas Number." Write any old thing and send it along, it may not be used but it may be useful.

THE EDITOR.

THE BURNING QUESTION.

Three Tommies sat in a trench one day,
Discussing the war, in the usual way,
They talked of the mud, and they talked
of the Hun,
Of what was to do, and what had been
done,
They talked about rum, and—'tis hard
to believe—
They even found time to speak about
leave,
But the point which they argued from
post back to pillar
Was whether Notts County could beat
Aston Villa.
—o—o—o—
The night sped away, and zero drew
nigh,
Equipment made ready, all lips getting dry,
And watches consulted with each passing
minute
Till five more to go, then 'twould find
them all in it ;
The word came along down the line to
" get ready ! "
The sergeants admonishing all to keep
steady,
But out rang a voice getting shriller and
shriller :
" I tell yer Notts County can beat Aston
Villa ! "

The Earth shook and swayed, and the barrage was on
As they leapt o'er the top with a rush, and were gone
Away into Hunland, through mud and through wire,
Stabbing and dragging themselves through the mire,
No time to heed those who are falling en route
Till, stopped by a strong point, they lay down to shoot,
Then through the din came a voice :
    " Say, Jack Miller !
I tell yer Notts County can beat Aston Villa."

—o—o—o—

The strong point has gone, and forward they press
Towards their objective, in number grown less
They reach it at last, and prepare to resist
The counter-attack which will come through the mist
Of the rain falling steadily ; dig and hang on,
The word for support back to H.Q. has gone,
The air, charged with moment, grows stiller and stiller—
" Notts County's no earthly beside Aston Villa."

—o—o—o—

Two " Blighties," a struggle through mud to get back
To the old A.D.S. down a rough duck-board track,
A hasty field dressing, a ride in a car,
A wait in a C.C.S., then there they are :
Packed side by side in a clean Red Cross train,
Happy in hopes to see Blighty again,
Still, through the bandages, muffled,
    " Jack Miller,
I bet you Notts County can beat Aston Villa ! "

HAIG HARRIES THE HUNS.

—:o:—

BY OUR SPECIAL CORRESPONDENT
Mr. TEECH BOMAS.

—:o:—

At break of day the hunters are about, and Haig's harriers hourly harry the Huns. What though the saturated bosom of mother earth is but a yielding morass which clasps mortals by the thighs, and makes every endeavour at progress one long struggle against nature in her vilest mood. The gallant umpty umpth went on gamely struggling through conditions which would have driven Napoleon to a headlong flight from the field of battle, crying as he went, " A horse ! A horse ! What's the good of one anyway." Yet the lads from ——— struggled on and gained the crest of the ridge. I could tell a tale of one aeroplane which gamely flew and scattered hundreds of generals, advancing to the attack in motor cars, although both its wings had been blown off in the gale. I could tell you a tale of self-sacrifice surpassing anything in this or any other war, of how one man of the —shires stood on the shoulders of another to enable the third to climb on the shoulders of the top one and so reach the top of the mud and stop a counter attack. But why take up one deed when everything was epic. And so the battle rages, and Haig harries the Huns, though the heavens' rage and mother earth covers herself with Flanders vilest product. As I am going for my usual winter's tour to warmer climates after the end of Nov. there will be no more operations on a large scale to chronicle.

TEECH BOMAS.

OUR DIARY.

—o—o—o—

BY LIEUT. SAMUEL PEPYS.

—o—

On the Thursday of last week we did take up our residence in a new part of the trench. Tis a noisome place, and I am disgusted of it. The mud is of a terrifying stickiness, and I am feared for my breeches, which cost me one guinea at the Hope Brothers' establishment in Cheapside. Also I have spoiled my new coat on the barbed wire, which has grieved me, as it was of a good shape and fitting. Anne is also disturbing me much, as she is lavish in expenditure now, and writes me of coal which is now up 10/- the ton and potatoes, which I think she might forego, as they are of a great expense. One tells me that my old friend Major the Honourable Reginald is like to leave us. This grieves me, as to drink a stoop of ale with him was one of my few pleasures in this abominable country. It is raining with an intensity not to be believed, and our trench gets daily more unbearable. I think the Government should move in the matter, but one hears that they are taken up with other matters of lesser concern. Anne writes me that the enemy has again sent an airship to London, and has broken more windows. This is intolerable, and one must blame the Peelers. I did go to hear a speech on discipline yesterday, which did intrigue me mildly. It is said that Captain Hannay did throw a cricket ball 65 yards and did thus win many wagers. I saw the Countess of Kruisstraat in the Park yesterday, and was much impressed by her beauty and dressings. She was in the new style which is most becoming to her though I must tell Anne the mode would not suit her, as it is most expensive. As I must take a party out for the sandbagging, to bed at 7 of the clock, after a poor dinner, the Macconnochie being but of medium quality and not too hot.

TO MARIE,

—o—o—o—

You were very shy and gentle, and your
eyes were very blue,
And you didn't know (how could you?)
what I had seen you do;
For I paid my bill, without a word, and
went upon my way.
But this little recollection has diverted
many a day.
—:o:—
My coat was hanging by the door, it's
pockets gaping wide,
And I was dining far away—my table
was beside
The long gilt-beaded mirror, and so, my
fair Marie.
Although I did not try to yet I could
not fail to see.
—:o:—
You sniffed, when serving potage, and I
breathed a fervent wish,
That you wouldn't sneeze a second time
upon my plate of fish.
My coat was very near you, and you had
a cold I know,
For you snatched my handkerchief and
took a surreptitious blow.
—:o:—
Your little nose was very red—I saw it
in the glass—
I smiled—I smile again—you funny,
fascinating lass.
You know, how people meet in France—
we meet, we pay, we part:
But that day you stole my handkerchief,
you stole into my heart.

R.M.O.

THE WOOING OF EVANGELINE—

IN A SUPPORT LINE DUG-OUT.

—o—o—o—

Aloud, at nights, he will philosophise ;
And squeaks his senile counsel all the
day ;
Pedantic lover, old and grim and grey,
He mingles love with wisdom, when he
tries
To win his maid with sage remarks and
wise.
And though I often drive the pair away,
They still return, and then I hear him say,
With many coughs, and splutterings,
and sighs :

—o—o—o—

' The more I see of war, and all its woes,
The happier do I feel, Evangeline,
That you and I, dear heart, are not like
those
Poor devils there, who have to fight, my
Queen,
They have a rotten time, and Heaven
knows,
We're better off, us rats :—
    Some Pork and Bean ? "
        C.L.P.

WITH THE USUAL APOLOGIES.

—o—o—o—

If you can drink the beer the Belgians
sell you,
And pay the price they ask with ne'er a
grouse,
If you believe the tales that some will
tell you,
And live in mud with ground sheet for a
house.

If you can live on bully and a biscuit,
And thank your stars that you've a tot of
rum,
Dodge whizzbangs with a grin, and as
you risk it
Talk glibly of the pretty way they hum,
If you can flounder through a C.T. nightly
That's three-parts full of mud and filth
and slime,
Bite back the oaths and keep your jaw
shut tightly,
While inwardly you're cursing all the
time,
If you can crawl through wire and crump-
holes reeking
With feet of liquid mud, and keep your
head
Turned always to the place which you
are seeking,
Through dread of crying you will laugh
instead,
If you can fight a week in Hell's own
image,
And at the end just throw you down and
grin,
When every bone you've got starts on a
scrimmage,
And for a sleep you'd sell your soul
within,
If you can clamber up with pick and
shovel,
And turn your filthy crump hole to a
trench,
When all inside you makes you itch to
grovel,
And all you've had to feed on is a stench,
If you can hang on just because you're
thinking
You haven't got one chance in ten to live,
So you will see it through, no use in
blinking
And you're not going to take more than
you give,
If you can grin at last when handing over,
And finish well what you had well begun,
And think a muddy ditch a bed of clover,
You'll be a soldier one day, then, my son.

A LETTER FROM THE FRONT.

—:o:—

MY OWN, DEAREST SWEETHEART,—

I feel I cannot go on like this the uncertainty of it is driving me mad. Your letters hint but tell me nothing. Yet surely we should have no secrets after what has happened. At night I wake and my mind is one chaotic patchwork of questions, and yet no answer is possible. Can you imagine the suffering of this uncertainty. After those days together—what golden ones they were—this! To lie in a dug-out with a throbbing head, and the prey of any haphazard dread and uncertainty which may seize my disordered brain, Light of my life, remember all we have been to each other, that once your head has lain on my shoulder, and that your kiss has meant to me a paradise which had only perfect happiness and content, that your presence meant oblivion of the world and its meaner inhabitants, that your beauty left me stunned, yet satisfied that of the world I had seen its fairest flower, remember all this and in your next letter tell me, relieve my mind of this torturing anxiety which threatens the very foundations of my being, tell me, did you make that cake yourself?

Yours, to eternity,
HARRY.

Sentry! What of the night?
The sentry's answer I will not repeat,
Though short in words, 'twas with feeling
replete,
It covered all he thought and more,
It covered all he'd thought before,
It covered all he might think yet
In years to come. For he was wet
And had no rum.

Walking one day on a duckboard.
I was weary and ill at ease,
And my hands grasped vainly at nothing,
And the mud came up to my knees,
The duckboard began oscillating,
I knew that I had to go,
So I gave one wild and final plunge,
And fell in the mud below.

THE LAST STRAW.

—0—0—0—

Hear now the howl of rage which rends
The skies from Nieuport to Lorraine,
Which wanders down the line, and ends
When breath has flown, and all are sane;
Blanched faces, furtive looks and eyes
Which show the horror felt by all,
And fury at the sacrilege
Holds every one of us in thrall.

—:o:—

And in each heart the certainty
That soon the deed reward shall find,
Just, swift and sure the payment be,
And we to pity all are blind;
He, with this infamy has topped
A list of crimes which e'er must irk us,
Who with a craven hand has dropped
A bomb in Piccadilly Circus.

AS OF OLD.

— o—o—o —

And it came to pass that the King gathered together all his men, and his chariots, and his mules, and there was a great multitude gathered together, so that there was no blade of grass seen in the land. And one of the King's captains called WINDUP did send for his chief charoteer and did say unto him, " Bring unto me INTHA." Now INTHA was a man skilled in the learning of mules. And, lo, the chief charoteer brought INTHA unto WINDUP and did say unto him, " Lo, I have brought this man." And WINDUP spake and said, " It is given unto me to reward one man by sending him unto Blitee, a land flowing with milk and honey, and I have a good account of thee. Say, desirest thou to be the man chosen ? " And INTHA answered him and said, " Not-arf," which being interpreted, means " Yea, verily." And WINDUP, the captain of the King's host, said unto him, " Go thou to the river Ancre. and bathe there, and put on clean raiment, and return unto me, and I will give thee a parch- ment." And INTHA did even as he was bid, and bathed himself in the river Ancre, and was clean. And he went unto the keeper of clean raiment, and received divers articles as white as snow. And when he had girded up his loins with clean raiment, he returned unto WINDUP, the King's captain, and said unto him, " Lo, I have done as my lord commanded." And WINDUP, the captain, said unto him, " Lo, take the parchment, and go thou to Blitee, and thou shalt return here in ten days. And if thou returnest not, then shalt thou suffer divers pain and penalties even the punishment of Effpy of the order one, and thy house also shall suffer." And it came to pass that INTHA took the parchment, and travelled unto Blitee and sojourned there for the space of ten days. Now there was much wine there. And it came to pass that INTHA had a great feast before returning unto his captain, and he drank of the wine until he got " Blotto," which being interpreted m ans, " Possessed of an evil spirit," and he returned not. And it came to pass that WINDUP, the King's captain, did send two men of his bodyguard to fetch INTHA. And they brought him. And WINDUP, the captain, said unto him, " Wherefore didst thou not return unto me, but sojourned in Blitee for many days ? " And Intha answered him and said. " Lord I was sick " (and in this he spake the truth). And WINDUP said, " Wherefore then didst thou not go unto a man learned in such things, and obtain a parchment from him ? " And INTHA answered him not. And WINDUP, the captain, was exceeding wroth, and commanded them to take INTHA outside and do unto him the punishment which had been commanded. And it came to pass as he had said, and INTHA did get a dose of Effpy of the number 1 order and was chastened.

MORT POUR LA FRANCE.

—o—o—o—

Many the graves that lie behind the line,
Scattered like shells upon a blood-stained
strand,
Crosses and mounds, that eloquently
stand
To mark a spot, that forms some hero's
shrine.
And one, that nestles near a shattered
pine,
Beside a war-wrecked wall, in barren
land,
Is tended, daily, by a woman's hand,
Moistened by tears, that in her bright
eyes shine.

—o—o—o—

But proud she was, and proud she still
can be,
Lover and patriot, both, she proudly
reads
His epitaph. It dries her tears to know,
That he has purchased immortality :—
" Mort pour la France." He filled his
Country's needs,
And though he rests, for France he'd
have it so.

TO-DAY'S GOSSIP.

BADGES OF RANK.—When an officer
wears a trench coat it is impossible
to tell what his rank is. However,
I am told that a useful new regulation
provides for the wearing of rank badges
on the garment.—THE RAMBLER in the
" Daily Mirror."

Correspondence.

To the Editor,
" B.E.F. Times."
Sir,
I am surprised and pained to see
a letter in your valuable periodical
advocating the issue of Gin to Generals.
Sir, your correspondent must be most
unpatriotic—he may even be a " Bolo."
Those who have made a careful study of
such problems have quite definitely
proved that the minutest doses of alcohol
poison the body for at least two days,
and after the primary exhilaration, there
is a reaction—particularly the morning
after. Is it wise, sir, at a time like this
to run the risk of making our generals
too optimistic in the evening, and too
depressed in the morning ?
Yours Indignantly,
F. A. NATIC,
Hon. Sec. Little Stodgebury
Temperance Association.
P S.—I might suggest that if our
generals really need some stimulant,
they might do worse than try a mixture
in which I am interested—T.O. This
cordial, which stimulates and cheers,
but does not inebriate, was invented by
me specially to meet the case of those
who must have some stimulant, and any
profits I make out of it will go towards
furthering the campaigns of temperance
—and T.O.

—o—o—o—

To the Editor,
" B.E.F. Times."
Sir,
I wish to draw your attention to
the shameful way in which no mention is
made of the glorious Manxman in this
war. We hear about the glorious Anzacs
and Canadians—English county troops,
Scotch, Irish, Welsh, and so on, but I
have yet to see the gallant lads from the
Isle of Man mentioned. Sir, they have
done their bit with the best, and it is a
very galling business for them to feel that
their pluck is unnoticed. Trusting
that the publicity given to the matter by
means of your widely read paper will
remove the injustice.—I am,
Yours, etc ,
CALL HAINE.
BILGE VILLA, BUNKUM.

LATE NEWS FROM THE RATION DUMP.

— o — o — o —

Three submarines have been mined on the Menin Road. Crew of one captured.

— o — o — o —

The Swedes have declared war. Hence the shortage of turnips. Serious rumours that the Jamaicans are preparing for war and will cut off the rum issue.

— o — o — o —

The Germans have only 14 shells left.

— o — o — o —

Three flying pigs reached the Hun trenches. (This is probably an optimist rumour.)

— o — o — o —

The pay for men at the base is going to be doubled owing to the increased cost of living, and halved for those in the line as they are not in a position to spend it.

— o — o — o —

12 Zeppelins have been forced to descend, as we have discovered a new method of extracting gas from any distance.

TO-DAY'S GOSSIP.

A FRIEND of mine, a Staff Officer of considerable rank, informs me that many misunderstandings arise through the difficulty of distinguishing between officers of G and Q Branches of the Staff during the dark hours of night. Some genius of the War Office has, however, introduced a new order whereby members of G side will in future wear bright red pyjamas and those of Q bright green ones, thus overcoming a really serious difficulty.

EDITORIAL.

HERE we are, knocking the Xmas number into shape again. It certainly does not seem to be twelve months since we were engaged on the same job, and yet quite a lot seems to have happened in the interval. By the time this number is published we shall have been running for two years and the first volume (containing first 15 numbers) should have made its bow to (let us hope) a kind and uncritical public. This Xmas we are more ambitious, and are making an effort to fill 20 pages, and the success of the venture must depend on how our wild appeals for copy are received by units. Of course it's quite likely that this war business may interfere with our plans and disturb the even tenor of our ways, so that our readers will understand, should the number contain less than the advertised 20 pages, that we have had to drop the pen for the sword, and go and liberate some more French villages, and thus fight the demon of oppression and barbarism, the last remaining relics of bestiality, brutality and Kultur. Should it come to this then indeed is the knell of Germanic despotism sounded, as the Sub-Editor is a holy terror at the end of a sword, and should once it be forced into his hand then Heaven help Hindenburg, as no one else could. However, there seems to be no alternative, and the Publisher has written home for a new pair of spurs and a mess canteen, so that he is evidently considering the necessity of taking an active part in the quarrel at no very distant date. However, one hopes that we may be allowed to have Xmas in peace. We cannot close without giving one and all the old greetings. Here's a Happy Xmas and New Year to you all, and may next Xmas see the whole damned business over. We are laying six to four on.

THE EDITOR.

A CHRISTMAS TALE.

—o—o—o—

ALFRED Higgins was a soldier. Officially he was No. 249,921, Pte. Higgins, A. His conduct sheet showed that he had usually been present when F.P. was handed out. On Christmas morning Alfred, with others, was holding the line. It was one of those Christmas mornings with which we have grown so familiar in this war. All was peace and goodwill. The gas gongs were chiming out their message of joy to all mankind, and the merry bark of the pip squeak, aided by the staccato cough of the how., combined to give the necessary impression of all being right with the world. Alfred had fallen into a deep reverie, when his sergeant approached him and said, "Alfred, have you had any rum?" Alfred moodily said "No." "Well," said the sergeant cheerily, handing him a canteen full, "have mine!"

* * * * * * *

When Alfred recovered, he found his hand being stroked by a 'V.A.D.' in a base hospital

---

OUR DIARY.

—o—o—o—

By LIEUT. SAMUEL PEPYS.

—o—

RUMOUR has come that our men have attacked the enemy with much vigour in Picardy, and have dealt grievously with him. This is of a good hearing, as last week he did annoy us much by throwing at us grenades of a great size, and again with some poisonous vapours. I did witness a game of hockey this last week, and was much amused at the efforts of many of the players, who did stop to cough frequently. The Countess of Cambrai was there, and all the beaux were much taken by her appearance, she being dressed in the latest mode and of Paris. Indeed, one does hear that there was fighting at Crockfords after dinner about her. I am glad Anne is not over in this country, otherwise it might give the most extravagant ideas to her, and there are many reasons that she is better in England. I took the coach with a merry party to A—— the other day, and we did enjoy ourselves much. All the young females of the town were to be seen, and one notices not too much of bashfulness. I am glad Anne is in England, as it is very wet in this country. Everything is of the most expensive, and soda is up one penny on the bottle, so that one must be careful. I did notice some strange soldiers this last week, and have been told they were from the Americas. They were of a goodly presence, but of a most ununderstandable language, talking, it seemed to me, much through the nose. As I must go on patrol soon, to bed at 8 of the clock, in a bad mood and with the megrims, as I am wet and the rum did not come up to-night.

TO THOSE AT HOME.

Lift up your heads, O ye people, and
be ye lifted up, ye everlasting grousers,
and so will ye help in what is yet to do.

—o—o—o—

Ye who have given so freely nor counted
cost,
Given of money and time ye could spare;
Give once again, give us what we would
have the most,
Out of your confidence give us a share.

—o—o—o—

Though there be many whose faith ne'er
can shaken be
Steadfast through all, be it good, be it ill,
Others whose faith veers with each wind
alternately
Voicing, unheeding, their doubtings at
will.

—o—o—o—

Yet every doubt that is whispered through
heedlessness
Pulls twice its weight, and the harm
still remains,
Going the rounds, growing rather to
more than less,
Redoubling losses and carping at gains.

—o—o—o—

Lift up your heads, that in you our new
strength we find,
Give of your faith as ye give of your gold,
Doubtings and fears all forgotten and
left behind,
So shall ye help us most now, as of old,

—o—o—o—

Hush all the whisperers voicing in
thoughtless way,
Reckoning little the harm that they do,
Steadfast in truth go ye onward from
day to day,
Trusting in us and we trusting in you.

IN MY GARDEN.

—o—o—o—

WITH APOLOGIES TO THE "DAILY MIRROR,"

—o—

Although Crows' Feet are usually sown
later in the season, in many sectors
where a warm sunny border of light soil
is available, the seed of this useful
vegetable may, with advantage, be got
in at this date.

—§ † §—

Where the soil is damp and heavy, an
early planting of gooseberries is attended
with some risk. This hardy perennial,
being a strong grower, will quickly
cover an unsightly patch of waste
ground The best crops of this luscious
fruit have been obtained when some
support has been given by stakes.

—§ † §—

It must be remembered that the
planting of Toffee-apples on the border
of your neighbour's allotment will
seriously interfere with the ripening of
his gooseberries.

—§ † §—

By this time berms should be well
covered with a luxuriant crop of Mustard
and Cresol.

—§ † §—

That aggravating insect, the Phlying
pig (sus maximus fossae) is particularly
voracious just now, and can only be
kept under by a liberal use of the
vermoral sprayer. Should vermoral
solution be unobtainable, an excellent
substitute can be made by stirring a
scoopful of chloride of lime in a tea-
spoonful of water. This solution can be
safely stored in water carts for an
indefinite period.

ART. A. XERXES.

THE TOAST OF THE IRREPRESSIBLE.

The Colonel, the Major, the Adjutant,
the whole of the Regiment's Mess
Were talking of Germans, of Ships, and
of Things, of up-to-date War and
the trouble it brings ;
And they wished they were back once
more, to the slack, old days of the
good Queen Bess ;

—o—o—o—

When Raleigh and Drake had manned
their ships, and made the foemen run,
And returned, in a trice, to their worship-
ping home, scattering money and
silvery foam,
The gifts of the seas, where their victories
over Spanish fleets were won.

—o—o—o—

The Subaltern rose, a toast to propose:—
" Why should we worry or grieve ;
And damn those silly old days," he said,
as he shook his curly, precocious
head,
" There are men like these, to-day, on
the seas, to carry us home on leave.
So here's to the boat, where'er she float,
that takes our soldiers over,
A health to the ship, that makes the trip,
to Folkestone or to Dover."

—o—o—o—

And unafraid of the stir he made, he
cried, " Don't think I'm silly—
Let the enemy gas us, and bomb us, and
strafe ; we can give him as good as
we get—not half !
If once a year, we can get out o' here, to
the lights o' Piccadilly."

The Colonel recalled his familee ; and
he wanted his leave once more.
The portrait, they say, of the Major's
wench, hangs in his dugout in
Canada Trench ;
And he couldn't guess, if she would say
yes, next time, that he talked it o'er.

—o—o—o—

The Adjutant, Brown, wore a pessimist's
frown—of " Private Affairs " he
vaunted,
Of a moribund aunt, who was lingering
still ; and a hope, that he'd head off
the rest in her will.

—o—o—o—

But the Subaltern, bad, was a light-
headed lad, and everyone knew
what he wanted,
He was just a bit wild, and he beamed
and he smiled, as he toasted the
Leave Boat again ;
He sprang to his feet, and he stepped on
the toe, of his most apoplectic and
gouty C.O.
Whose remark does not matter—'twas
drowned in the chattering Subaltern's
ribald refrain
Of " Here's to the boat, where'er she
float, that takes our soldiers over,
A health to the ship, that makes the trip
to Folkestone or to Dover."

R.M.O.

A SPLASH OF COLOUR.

In variegated colours, rich and new
Artists may dabble ; poets love to sing
Of dragon flies, with iridescent wing,
That dazzle with their brightness every hue
Of art ; of rainbows, in a drop of dew ;
Of butterflies, at morning, fluttering
Above the rarest flowers ; the priceless
string
Of jewels. All are fair, but none will do.
—:0:—
For multicoloured metaphors, I grope
Climbing a long kaleidoscopic scale,
Striving to do you justice, but I fail.
Nor, in a sonnet, can I ever hope
To paint the incandescence of your voice—
Your language, R.S.M., is far too choice.

C.L.P.

LONG AGO.

BY GILBERT FRANKAU.

To-day, as we drank our wine,
                    Editor mine !
I thought of the early days,
                    Long ago ;
When, new to soldier-ways,
                    We didn't know
That a G.O.C. was different from a third
          grade G.S.O.

—o—o—o—

I thought about Shoreham Camp—
                    Devilish damp !
Of the blue that he used to wear—
                    The recruit ;
And the swears that he used to swear
                    When this " loot "
Took the early morning route march
          (only, then, we called it " root." ;

—o—o—o—

Of our Div. as it used to be,
                    In K 3 ;
Of the faces of damn good chaps
                    One might meet
('Neath funny hard service caps)
                    On the street
Near the Hippodrome at Brighton with
          a piece of something sweet ;

—o—o—o—

Of days when we all were green,
                    In 'fourteen ;
Of tents that were bare of boards ;
                    And the rain ;
And the cockneys (as tight as lords)
                    In the train
Rolling home from week-end passes back
          to Shoreham Camp again ;

Of drills that I used to drill
                    On the hill,
Rather bucked but deuced shy
                    At command,
'Neath the Sergeant-Major's eye,
                    Book-in-hand ;
And of how the Buffs outswanked us
          with the first battalion band.

—o—o—o—

Lord, those other days they seem
                    Like a dream—
Movies flashed upon a screen
                    Long ago ;
Like some half-remembered scene
                    From a show
That one went to half-seas-over and
          whose name one doesn't know.

—o—o—o—

Where are those days to-day ?
                    Editor, say !
Where are those blue-clad men ? . . .
                    I suppose
One meets with them now and then—
                    N.C.O.'s
With their Don C. Emma's scarlet faded
          to a washed-out rose.

—o—o—o—

Where are the lads who drank,
                    Full of swank,
In the halls of the Metropole ?
                    Does one find
Here and there a cheery soul
                    To remind
Of the pegs we drank together and the
          girls we left behind ?

—o—o—o—

What's the good in harking back
                    Along a track
That we travelled three years ago—
                    Rather more !
Let's wait till the last best " show " ;
                    Wipe the floor
With the Hun ; take off our gum-boots,
          and return our guns to store ;

Then, the fellows who took the job
           At a bob
While the blighters who wouldn't fight
           Grabbed the dough !)
Will have one great old night . . . .
           And I know
That they'll talk till early morning of
    " the days of long ago."

10/12/17.

—:o:—

Little things we want to know
Why messages by pigeon go ?
The eagle bird can fly as high
And C.O.'s dote on pigeon pie !

—:o:—

Why the man with one inch group
Joined the Ancient Archie Troupe ?
Surely it would raise a smile
If he grouped below a mile !

—:o:—

Why patrols with books to sign
Wander up and down the line ?
Surely flanks would safer be
If Fritz endorsed my 153 !

—:o:—

Why, although I've studied war
For a brace of years or more,
At present I can not secure
A case of Walker or of Dewar ?

—:o:—

Why—but stay ! I'm indiscreet,
Rushing in with careless feet
Where the angels fear to tread—
I nearly tried to pot " the red."

Red hair and freckles, legs beneath the
    lace
Of Sunday petticoats, long legs and
    slender,
That strength and leverage, oft-times,
    would lend her
In scaling trees ('tis true, without much
    grace,
But lots of skill) and wildly kick in space,
As she hung poised from topmost
    branches tender,
Before she dropped ; whereafter she
    would mend her
Bedraggled hose, with grave unblushing
    face.

—o—o—o—

She speaks—a goddess tall and fair and
    stately —
" Why Jack, we haven't seen each other
    lately ;
Not since you went to France." My
    sacred aunt !
Tempus et bellum omnia mutant ;
But this their greatest change.—I scratch
    my napper,
Can this be Phyllis, that unholy flapper ?
             C.L.P.

Sing a song of Christmas !
Pockets full of slush,
Four and twenty P.B.I.
A dixey full of " mush,"
When that dixey opened
The Tommies said " Oh my !
It's beef to-day by way of change "
And then began to cry.

WHY NOT ?

—o—o—o—

We've had a play in ragtime, and we've
    had a ragtime band,
We've had a ragtime army, and we've
    had a ragtime land ;
But why not let us have what we have
    never had before ?
Let's wade right in tomorrow and let's
    have a ragtime war.

—:o:—

Let's carry up our duckboards to a
    ragtime's jerky strains,
Let's whistle ragtime ditties while we're
    bashing out Hun-brains,
Let's introduce this melody in all we say
    and do,
In our operation orders, and in all our
    lies to Q.

—:o:—

Let us write O.O.'s to music, and the
    red-hats can decide
The witching hour of zero to a dainty
    Gaby Glide,
We'll take the fateful plunge, and when
    we venture o'er the top,
We'll do it to a Turkey Trot or tuneful
    Boston Hop.

—:o:—

We'll drink our S.R.D. to tune, and even
    " chatting up "
Becomes a melody in rhyme if done to
    " Dixie Pup,"
A bombing raid to " Old Kentuck "
    would make a Fritzie smile,
He'd stop a bomb with pleasure to a
    ragtime's mystic guile.

—:o:—

Can you see our giddy " Q " staff, as
    they go up to the line,
Just walking round the trenches to the
    air " Kentucky Mine,"
Gaily prancing down the duckboards, as
    they tumble o'er a bucket,
To the quiet seducing strains of " My
    Dear Home in Old Kentucket."

From Intelligence Summaries.

———:o:———

OPERATIONS.—At 1·2 a.m. a patrol
of 1 O.R. left our wire where it was, and
retired to his dug-out. No enemy was
seen.

—o—o—o—

ARTILLERY.—1·10 p.m. to 2·3 p.m.
Our front and support lines were heavily
shelled with 303 inch shrapnel. No
direct hits were obtained.

—o—o—o—

RIFLE AND M.G. FIRE.—Sniper
suspected at A 29, Q 21 3/4, 4 1/8. (See
Artillery above.

—o—o—o—

T.M.'s.—Our H.T.M.'s fired one
round rapid at suspected enemy Pigeon
Emplacements.

—o—o—o—

MOVEMENT.—11·28 a.m. Man seen
walking along pathway running E.S.W.
from N.S.E. corner of M——— Wood. He
was carrying a dark brown spherical
object with a mottled surface, on a white
disc. This seems to point to an early
Christmas.

2·3 p.m.—Sentry with head and
shoulders above parapet at B 73, h 19
1/4, 7 1/2. Our " heavies " were
informed, and fired a concentration of 31
rounds at 8 p.m. The sentry was
enveloped by a cloud of dust and small
stones. Our observer was hit by a flying
tunic button, and after the shoot a boot
and part of a rifle were seen lying about
30 yards from the point where the sentry
had stood. A hit is claimed.

—o—o—o—

MISCELLANEOUS.—1·4 a.m. Two
rockets emitting a pale black light were
sent up in quick succession from M 19, n
50, 40. No action followed.

—o—o—o—

ENEMY'S ATTITUDE. Distinctly
hostile.

AS OF OLD.

—o—o—o—

AND it came to pass that divers men were needed to labour in the land, so that the King's hosts might journey to the Land of the Amalekites. And they sent for those skilled in the art of digging and delving, and said unto them "Go ye and prepare the way for us." And men to the number of fifty girded up their loins, and they took spades and weapons, and tin hats they took also. And one of them, by name SAPPA, the son of ARREB, did quake exceedingly when he heard the tumult that there was in the place, for the Amalekites did have an up-wind, and raged furiously. And it came to pass that SAPPA, the son of ARREB did say to his Captain "Lo, I am not afraid, but I am suffering from a palsy." And the Captain said unto him "Get thee back, and tell the leech what thou hast told me, and peradventure he will give thee a potion, which will drive out the palsy." And he went. And when he had come unto Rap, where the leech dwelt, he went in unto him and made much lamentation, and said, "Lo, thy servant is stricken with a palsy, and the blood is like water in my veins." And the leech said unto him "Beware, oh SAPPA, that thou deceivest me not." And SAPPA answered him and said "Lo, my speech is as the speech of babes and sucklings, and there is no guile in my tongue." Then did the leech make much examination, and he went away and thought for a space. And when he had come back he did write on the parchment N.Y.D., which being interpreted means "No you don't," and he gave unto SAPPA a potion of Kasteroil. And he sent a messenger to the Captain, and he said "Lo the feet of SAPPA are cold, and it behoveth him to labour like Tumen, and peradventure

he will not again suffer with a palsy. And the Captain tied SAPPA to the wheels of his chariot, and left him for a space. And then he said unto him, "Thou wilt now labour like Tumen, lest a worse thing befall thee." And SAPPA did as he was bid, and the palsy left him, and he was cured. And the fame of it went right through the King's hosts, as is written in the Second Book of Battorders.

AUNT ANNIE'S CORNER.

—o—o—o—

TENDER TALKS TO TINY TOTS.

—o—o—

MY DEAR TOT-TIES,

A ver-y hap-py X-mas to you all, and I hope you all en-joy the nice pres-ents that Sant a Claus brings you. Sant-a Claus has told me what some of you will find in your stock-ings. Lit-tle Wil-lie Poile is go-ing to get a tick-et col-lect-or's out-fit with green and yell-ow rail-way tick-ets. I hope he will be kind, and let the oth-er lit tle boys use them.

—:o:—

LIT TLE Al-fie Stalk-er has got a nice box of bricks, and a set of Mech-ano, and now he will be able to make some nice forts and things for his sold-iers.

—:o:—

LIT-TLE Fer-die Ad ams is get-ting a wool-ly lamb on a nice green stand, and a duck to float in his bath. Wouldn't you like to see him play ing with it?

—:o:—

BIL-LIE Tween-ey is go ing to have a box of paints, and I ex-pect he will have great fun with them; per-haps he will be ab-le to make a lot of things look dif-fer-ent from what they real-ly are, which would be very clev-er, would-n't it?

Your Lov-ing
AUNT ANNIE.

Correspondence.

To the Editor,
"B.E.F. Times."

Sir,

I read in the papers that a star is being granted for the men who fought in 1914. As one of the earliest conscientious objectors (I discovered my conscience on August 5th, 1914) I must ask you to obtain for us some especial recognition. Surely you cannot but admire the struggle we have put up against the overstrong odds of a sensitive conscience, and that we have been. defeated is no fault of ours. We trust that you will be able to help us in the matter.

I am, Sir,
Yours etc.,
ANASTASIUS DUNN,
Bowler Villa, Feltham.

To the Editor,
"B.E.F. Times."

Sir,

While waiting in a queue with my rum card the other night I was rudely approached by a sergeant, and told to "Getterlongoutervit." I protested, but eventually submitted to the hectoring importunities of one placed over me by a social upheaval. Surely this is not the spirit which will win the war, and I maintain that the sergeant had no right to speak to me in so unceremonious a manner, even if I HAD had one issue already, and merely taken my place in the queue on the chance that it might come off.

I am, Sir,
Yours etc.,
WILLIAM SHIFTER.

ANSWERS TO CORRESPONDENTS.

TROUBLED, TOOTING BEC.—When you have filled up your sugar card truthfully and well, destroy it, and a new one will be issued next week.

—o—o—o—

ENQUIRER.—No. A policeman riding round the streets exhibiting a notice saying "Take Cover" is NOT encouraging your predatory instincts, but advising you to leg it for the nearest hole.

—o—o—o—

TOMMY.—Yes. If you hang your sock over the parapet on Xmas Eve you are likely to get something in it—or you—when you go to fetch it.

—o—o—o—

Owing to lack of space other answers to our numberless correspondents are unavoidably held over.

Will It Come Off?

—o—o—o—

HERE we have William Hohenzollern with a busted flush trying to choke off a crowd with a full house, and trying to do it "on tick" ! ! !

THE OLD FIRM!
TWEN, TEFORTH AND CO.
Under Entirely New Management.

This Eminent Firm of General Merchants begs to announce to its Clients that, under the New Management, the following Additional Departments will be inaugurated :

THEATRE TICKET DEPARTMENT,
DANCING ACADEMY,
DAIRY DEPARTMENT and, a bit later,
FARMING AND SEEDS DEPARTMENTS.

—o—o—o—o—

" Like our friend, Sir Rosslyn Wemyss,
We are sound in all our schemyss."

—o—o—o—o—

We hope for the support which has been given so readily in the past, and every effort will be made to meet the wishes of clients.

Telephone, 20 lines : " 102, Museum."   Telegrams : " Hay and Kew."

GREAT SERIES OF LECTURES
WILL TAKE PLACE AT
"DEAD HUN FARM."

THE FOLLOWING HAVE PROMISED TO SPEAK :—

Sir SHETLAND STEDDES—Subject :
" What shall we do with our boys "

—o—o—o—o—

Mr. BARNES,
" The Labour-er- is worthy of his hire."

—o—o—o—o—

Mr. BENVER HAY,
" The blessings of Universal Peace."

—o—o—o—o—

Mrs. F. O. O. D. HUNTER,
On " Queues and their customs.'

—o—o—o—o—

NO SEATS RESERVED.

—o—o—o—o—

As there is likely to be a great demand for places, those who wish to hear these Lectures are advised to come early. Zero, 7.30 p.m. S.O.S , 10 p.m. Stretchers, 10 30 p.m.

160

THE B.E.F. TIMES.

WITH WHICH ARE INCORPORATED

The Wipers Times, The "New Church" Times The Kemmel Times & The Somme-Times.

No 5. Vol. 2.   Tuesday, January 22nd, 1918.   Price 1 Franc.

EDITORIAL.

1918. " SECONDS out of the Ring. Last round coming up." We have it on the best authority that William Hohenzollern has a little boat ready, with steam up. to cut it to Sweden. It came from the most reliable ration dump so naturally must be true. Up to now the luck has generally been with the Huns, but it looks as if it were going to leave them in the New Year. Anyway, we strongly advise Mr. Lloyd George and Sir Douglas Haig to get up and walk round their chairs three times. The sight of winter's white mantle always makes us feel poetic, but the thought of the future when the damned stuff melts restrains any rhapsodies on the subject. We have heard so many tales from Hunland about what he's going to do to us now that he has fixed Russia, that it makes us think he is trying to forget what we are going to do to him. It is still our firm opinion that any Hun could be bought for a tin of bully and a slice of bread. Anyway, we feel inclined to get mixed up with the prophets Elijah, John the Baptist and Horatio Bottomley, and prophecy the general bust up of the Hun at no very remote date. say September next, provided all pull their weight. This proviso is necessary, and does not apply only to those not in khaki. So here's to 1918, a speedy finish and a job well done. Here's the best of luck to you all in the New Year, and a quiet-thought and salutation to the memory of those stout lads who left us in the old.

THE EDITOR.

THOUGHTS.

I ain't no blooming Kipling, and I ne'er
    could be a Keats,
But I somehow sees a poem in whate'er
    I drinks and eats ;
When the night has fallen round me
    lovely verses seem to come,
As my thoughts in fancy linger on my
    evening tot of rum.

—o—o—o—

Oh ! Naught in Heaven's pellucid
    heights
When shadows play in Very lights,
Can stem the fervent words which come
Whene'er the sergeant drinks our rum.

—o—o—o—

There's a poem in a biscuit, there's a
    poem in our tea,
In fact the blooming rations make a book
    of poetry ;
But to have the gift to find it and to
    understand it fully,
One must learn to look for Khayyam in
    a blooming tin of bully.

—o—o—o—

For all the wine you drink, the lips you
    press,
Will only land you in some blooming
    mess,
And fourteen days of F.P. No. 1 :
But bully's bully, neither more or less.

—o—o—o—

You can have your blooming Shelley,
    Browning too, what did they know ?
They could only see a poem in the way
    the daisies grow ;
Had I got five francs to bet 'em then I'd
    very quickly risk it
That they couldn't find a poem in a
    blooming Army biscuit.

—o—o—o—

Hard is my lot, and hard is the world,
Hard are the shells day and night at us
    hurled,
Hard is the pavé, and hard is a stone,
But for hardness the biscuit's a class on
    its own.

TO THE AUTHORS OF Q 99065.

—o—o—o—

Brighter than tropic sunlight is the
    glare
Of the Brass Hats, of whom I speak ;
Redder than apples on the rustic cheek
Of winsome maidens, at the Country
    Fair,
The tabs and hat-bands, that these
    stalwarts wear ;
Rippling in wavelets, like some rapid
    creek ;
Or scented, smooth, immaculate and
    sleek,
The glossy beauty of their parted hair ;

—o—o—o—

Outrivalling the Cherry Blossom King,
Their boots, their belts, their buttons—
    everything
Most radiant. I dare not criticise
Their questions. And the foolscap query
    lies
Before my wondering gaze—I vainly
    strive
To answer their Q 99065.

                    C.L.P.

A Wail.

—o—o—o—

Life has many disappointments,
Days are never free from care,
For in spite of using ointments
Steadily I'm losing hair.

Another Wail.

—o—o—o—

Oh Mr. Cox ! Oh Mr. Cox !
My heart you've nearly broken,
By telling me I'm on the rocks.
In words most harshly spoken.

—§ † §—

You say that I have overdrawn
A sum quite awe-inspiring,
If that were all I would not mourn,
Nor would I be perspiring.

—§ † §—

But to these awful words you add
A legend disconcerting,
In large black print, which makes me sad,
My tender feelings hurting.

—§ † § -

Your envelope, in words of fire,
Inscribed, " Buy War Bonds NOW ! "
My dear old Cox just send a wire
And tell me, tell me, HOW ?

BILL SHAKESPEARE.

K.R.

—o—

Life in the Army, you must know
Is hedged about with Regulation,
And I suppose it must be so
Although it causes much vexation;
We have to mind each P and Q
So that our conduct shall not jar,
But always be conforming to
K.R.

—o—o—o—

This volume we must know off pat,
With all its manifold restrictions
Of para this and para that,
Not wholly free from contradictions;
Each separate ruling we must note,
For all good soldiers always are
At any time prepared to quote
K.R.

—o—o—o—

It deals with every sort of case,
A most complete encyclopedia ;
Its rules for every time and place
The soldier man may always read here;
Thus it will readily be seen
Why no excuses ever are
Accepted, when we contravene
K.R.

—o—o—o—

The powers who sit enthroned on high
Maintaining splendid isolation,
Draft an occasional A.C.I.
And publish it for information ;
Yet is our Bible and our Creed,
Our Lodestone, and our Guiding Star
On which we model every deed
K.R.

—o—o—o—

O shades of Authors past and gone
Whose works we read with admiration,
Inspiring those who labour on
To toil of keenest emulation,
O peerless Lore, and priceless Myth,
Careers in Arms you'll sternly mar,
If they're not in accordance with
K.R.

MINOR KEY.

D——

BY GILBERT FRANKAU.

[Being a plain statement of a disgusting crime wrought by the EDITOR of the "B.E.F. Times"; who ALTERED the last three lines of GILBERT FRANKAU's poem "Long Ago" in such a way as to make him appear guilty of writing false quantities.]

—o—o—o—

Waking, at noon, from nightmared
    slumber,
  I found beside my bed,
Your special Christmas Double Number—
  The which I duly read . . .
  And wished that I were dead.

—o—o—o—

Since that there is within its pages
  Which hurls my furious soul
From one rage into several rages ;
  And sends my self-control
  Completely ' up the pole.'

—o—o—o—

So that I swear, with long black curses,
  Never again to send
A single copy of my verses
  To you . . . who ought to spend
  Ten years in jail, my friend !

—o—o—o—

For you have had the nerve to " edit "
  On some amazing plan,
The lines which GILBERT "dono dedit"—
  And now, confound it, man,
  Those lines don't even scan !

—o—o—o—

Had you forged cheques, committed
    arson,—
  My clumsy Pioneer—
Rifled a church, or thrashed a parson,
  Or—drunk on Belgian beer—
  Sandbagged a Brigadier ;

One might have found extenuation,
  For these be minor crimes,
Compared with any alteration
  Made by a " Wipers Times "
  In GILBERT FRANKAU's rhymes :

—o—o—o—

For which black outrage, sin, and scandal
  Do I here, publicly,
Brand you a metre-murdering Vandal,
  And warn posterity :
  " He dared to edit ME."

6/1/18.

IN JUSTIFICATION.

—o—o—o—

Dear GILBERT, once again we don—
  To show our deep contrition—
Sackcloth and ashes. Hope is gone,
  You hate our new rendition.

—:o:—

We know the fact we altered it
  Calls for some explanation,
Although you're " nascitur non fit."
  Yet we've a reputation.

—:o:—

The line we gently camouflaged
  Presaged times alcoholic,
Right on our tend'rest corn you barged,
  Our instincts are bucolic.

—:o:—

Nights wild and woolly you impute
  To one, who seldom takes beer,
This imputation to refute
  We'd "edit" WILLIAM SHAKESPEARE.

—:o:—

Yet now to calm a poet's soul—
  And eke to get more "copy "—
We grovel in the ashes, coal,
  And own our line WAS sloppy.

THE EDITOR.

WHAT MIGHT HAVE BEEN.

—o—o—o—

THERE has been so much talk about poets produced by the War that I have lately given much thought to another side of the picture, and have wondered what would have happened if the War had coincided with several well-known poets. The following are a few of my deductions.

We will begin with Mr. W. Shakespeare, a poet who had a reputation, and flourished about the time of Queen Elizabeth. One can imagine him sitting in his dug-out near Hell-Fire Corner and writing thus :—

SCENE :—ESTAMINET AT DICKEBUSCH.

(ENTER TWO TOMMIES.)

TOMMY.—" Beer, mamselle, compree, what ? "

WAITRESS.—" Nutting doin'."

ATKINS.—" Narpoo ! Owell then get some old vang blang ! "

WAITRESS.—" No got it, m'sieur, you 'ave some vin rouge."

TOMMY.—" Alrite Bill, promenay out of this place,

We'll click at Café Belge for beer and cheese ;

This 'staminet's a dud. Alley—tout sweet ! "

ATKINS.—" Righto ! Cheero mamselle. Apree le guer ? "

(EXIT TOMMIES.)

Of course this is only a short example but space is limited.

Next we will take Craig, a poet who had a vogue in Surrey. The influence of War would have been felt by him thus :—

The Middlesex boys then took the field,
All full of knowing tricks ;
The blighted Hun he would not yield,
So they hit him for six.

Then take Browning, perhaps he might have felt the atmosphere thus :—

Teach me dearest Sergeant,
Don't look glum.
You may eat my bully,
Drink my rum.

—:o:—

Meet if you but ask it
Both desires,
Join a working party,
Put up wires.

—:o:—

And, where'er we be, dear,
Do fatigues ;
I am on F.P., dear,
Leagues and leagues.

Then again take a poet who had a reputation in Scotland, whether for poetry or some other vice is obscure. He naturally would have figured a Highlander in kilts. (I am not going to guarantee the spelling):—

O, Thamas is a wee puir body,
Thamas is a leear,
He draigl't a' his wee bit kilt,
Coming thro' the wire.

—:o:—

Gin a body meet our Thamas,
Thamas he can swear,
For he's draigl't a' his kilties
Coming thro' the wear.

This is easy, as you only have to alter the spelling of the word to make it fit. I could go on a long time, but this is the last page to be filled, and the Staff is waiting.

Correspondence.

To the Editor,
"B.E.F. Times."

Sir,

The other day during my journey from London to here on returning from leave, I gave the matter considerable thought. The following are a few of the suggestions I should like to put forward. Whether it would not be shorter and more comfortable to go via New York, San Francisco, Japan, Brindisi and Genoa. Also why only allow eight persons in a compartment, surely twelve could get in. Of course we can have no quarrel with the arrangement that anyone who has been travelling in the "Train de Luxe" (better known as the "Flying Scotchman") for five or six days, is unable to get a drink, as it's always after hours when the train arrives anywhere. This is quite right, as it might lead to undue hilarity, and prevent the pessimism necessary to thoroughly enjoy the journey.

I am, Sir,
Yours, etc.,
VOYAGEUR.

—o—o—o—

To the Editor,
"B.E.F. Times."

Sir,

The other day while waiting in a beer queue at the "Foresters Arms," I noticed many who were certainly not fit to wait perhaps hours in the cold. It is a scandal that these poor weaklings should be allowed to run the risk of trench feet just for a spot of beer. Surely something can be done to stop it, as often I have to wait a long time before getting any beer, and sometimes it is finished before I can get my elbow on the counter. I appeal to you to use your influence to get something done in the matter.

Yours Faithfully,
A. SAPPER.

A Few Things We Really Want to Know.

—o—o—o—

Having heard so much of what "Labour" will allow the Army to do—whether it isn't time we heard what the Army will allow Labour to do?

? ? ?

Whether it wouldn't be beneficial if many people—including Labour leaders—followed Mr. LLOYD GEORGE's lead, and read the "Wipers Times"?

? ? ?

Whether it might not give them a sense of proportion?

? ? ?

How much it would take to buy Turkey, lock, stock and barrel, at the present moment?

? ? ?

Whether the largely advertised Hun offensive hasn't put the wind up the Huns themselves more than anyone else? (With perhaps one exception.)

? ? ?

Whether the masses at home are not making an imaginary condition of food shortage themselves?

? ? ?

And why on earth they WANT margarine? (It's filthy stuff!)

ANSWERS TO CORRESPONDENTS.

Owing to lack of space, answers to our numberless correspondents are unavoidably held over.

NO TRENCH COMPLETE WITHOUT ONE.

—o—o—o—

OUR NEW PATENT DEVICE.

"Kamooflage"

GUARANTEED TO BAFFLE THE ENEMY

—o—o—o—

Buy one and try.

—o—o—o—

A GRATEFUL CUSTOMER WRITES :— "Sometime ago I bought one of your "Kamooflages" for my trench. This has been so successful that the Huns have mistaken it for a Staff College, and refrained from shooting at it. My nights are now undisturbed You may use this as you like.—THREE PIPS."

—o—o—o—

Send for one at once.

—o—o—o—

Kamooflage & Co ,
WYMEROO.

CAN YOU SKETCH ?

—o—o—o—

Sketching is the latest fad of the Army, and many are coining millions out of their dud productions,

WHY DON'T YOU?

Copy any well-known picture in the National Gallery and send it along to me. (The copy not the picture, as you might get nabbed) I'll then tell you how bad it is. If it's hopeless I shall recommend one of my 100 guinea courses (payment in advance), after which I'll guarantee to get you taken up by " The Slybander." Also you might write a play

—o—o—o—

Write in all cases to

John Cassell's Art Academy,

LONDON

Telegraphic Address—" Perhaps."

DO YOU LIKE BALLOONING ?

—o—o—o—

IF SO WRITE TO

"SAUSAGE," FRANCE,

AND ALL ARRANGEMENTS WILL BE MADE.

—o—o—o—

THIS FIRM IS FAMOUS FOR THE RAPIDITY OF ITS DESCENTS.

—o—o—o—

PARACHUTING A SPECIALITY.

—o—o—o—

SPLENDID SCENERY AND VIEW OF WAR TAKING PLACE IN THE DISTRICT.

o—o—o—

MOTOR TRIPS ARRANGED,

—o—o—o—

" In this awful pitch and toss age, Don't omit to try a sausage."

—o—o—o—

Charges Moderate.

Can You Wait ?

—o—o—o—

IF NOT, WHAT IS THE GOOD OF YOUR JOINING UP IN A QUEUE ?

—o—o—o—

We Give Instructions.

—o—o—o—

5 GUINEA COURSE OF 6 LESSONS AFTER WHICH WE GUARANTEE YOU WILL BE ABLE TO WAIT ANYWHERE.
ALSO THERE'S A CHANCE OF " WAITING " TILL THE WAR'S OVER. THUS AVOIDING INQUISITIVE TRIBUNALS.

—o—o—o—

" If you're single and A 1, Come and learn to wait, my son."

—o—o—o—

WRITE :—

Cuthbert & Slacker,
ENGLAND.

WHY??? LET THE HUNS WIN THE WAR AFTER THE WAR?

THEY ARE PREPARING BY MEANS OF A TRENCH UNIVERSITY. ALL RANKS CAN TAKE POST-GRADUATE COURSES, AND KEEP THEIR BRAINS ACTIVE, IN FACT,

THEY Are acquiring useful knowledge while, **YOU** are only studying C.R.O., and similar periodicals. WHAT YOU WANT—and must have—is your own series of lectures.

—o—o—o—o—

TO THIS END——US.

—o—o—o—o—

MARCH 3rd.—" SHELLS. What they are. Their uses. How to find them. Having found them, how to use the field dressing, etc , etc."
By Professor W. I. Z. BANGS, R.A., etc.

MARCH 10th.—" ALCOHOL AND ITS TERRIBLE RAVAGES. With particular reference to the wicked issue of rum to the troops "
By Professor T. T. BILGE, H_2O.

(THIS IS EXPECTED TO BE A VERY POPULAR LECTURE, AND TO AVOID DISAPPOINTMENT YOU SHOULD BOOK EARLY,)

MARCH 17th.—" THE GREAT WAR ; and how we won it every year until the Germans had no more reserves left."
By Professor HILLARY BULLOCK.

MARCH 24th.—" THE GERMAN AT HOME. His culture. Kindly Nature. Chivalry. Is he one of Nature's gentlemen ? Etc., etc."
By Professor RAMESES SNOWDEN.

—o—o—n—o—

THE ANGLO-AMERICAN UNIVERSITY EXTENSION LECTURE SYNDICATE, ACTIVE SERVICE BRANCH.

Secretary : **S. U. M. NUTT.** Telegrams : " WATAHOPE, B.E.F."

DO NOT READ THIS!!!
UNLESS YOU HAVE A GIRL AT HOME.
—o—o—o—o—

If you have. of course. you want to send her a souvenir. WE can supply just the tasty little thing you want Thousands to choose from :—

GERMAN SHOULDER STRAPS : 1/- each	— —	10/- a dozen
DITTO, BLOODSTAINED : 1/6 each	— —	15/- a dozen
SHELL HOLES, COMPLETE : 50/- each		
DUCKBOARDS—ENGLISH : 5/- each		
DITTO GERMAN : 10/- each		
IRON CROSSES : 6d. a gross.		

OUR SPECIALITY : BULLETS CAREFULLY FIXED IN BIBLES (FOR MAIDEN AUNTS) PHOTOGRAPHS (FOR FIANCEES.)

—●—o—o—o—

" To please your best girl. it is clear,
You must procure a souvenir."

—o—o—o—o—

SOUVENIR MANUFACTURING COMPANY, CAMBRAI.

THE
B. E. F. TIMES.

WITH WHICH ARE INCORPORATED

The Wipers Times, The "New Church" Times, The Kemmel Times & The Somme-Times.

No 6. Vol. 2.   Tuesday, February 26th, 1918.   Price 1 Franc.

EDITORIAL.

WE almost feel inclined to commence our yearly song of Spring in this number, but remembering past seasons we refrain, and bottle it all up until our next, or next but one, number. The cognoscenti are using the warm spell to get some ploughing done, and there should be a reasonable chance that we are not the " spudless army " in the Summer. Anyway, we have got our farming experts detailed, and they are at present sorting the seed so that we run no risk of planting carrots upside down. The war seems to present the usual items of interest, and the Hun has rung his bell and blown his horn, since when he appears to have adopted the " you hit me first " attitude. Nations at war are very like individuals in a temper, but the Hun very much reminds one of a small boy with half-a-brick in his hand, and a large window near by. He'd love to do it if he could only be sure of getting away. We note many fresh innovations since our last number. Those who were soldiers before a certain date are getting a medal, others are getting more pay, and all are getting chevrons. How we've managed to sleep at night without chevrons all this time is one of the astounding features of the war. As a Tommy remarked when preparing to go over the top, " If only I'd got me bloomin' chevrings I'd die 'appy." Re the lesser but still interesting point of money, it is gratifying to see that the gulleless sub will be able to adopt a more arrogant manner when talking to Mr. Cox. Our own feelings on the subject are rather mixed as we seem to be left out in the cold. However, we can at least draw pictures of how nice it would have been if we'd had all that money when we were subs. To paraphrise an old classic :

When we were subs,

When we were subs,

When we were subs together ;

We drew but seven-and-six a day,

When we were subs together.

How ver, let the dead past bury its dead, Mr. Cox can afford to forgive and forget. Yet can we forget the furtive approach, the pleading eye and the plaintive request for a small overdraft, " only another tenner, I'm going over to-morrow." However, it is nice to have a lot of young Rothschilds for subs, and we elders can at least think we are mixing with "money." We are grateful for " copy " sent by newcomers to the Division, and extend them a welcome in real Oliver Twist style.

THE EDITOR.

THE BATTLE OF OXFORD STREET
BY " WOOLF."

Dear Germans list while I tell the tale
Of the awful battle in Oxford Street,
When the pavement shook, and the shops turned pale,
In the blood-bespatted—Oxford Street.

"STICK IT."

What matter though the wily Hun
With bomb, and gas and many a gun
In futile fury, lashes out,
Don't wonder what it's all about—
　　　　" Stick it."

—o—o—o—

When soaked in mud, half dead with cold,
You curse that you're a soldier bold ;
Don't heave your " A " frame through the night,
And, though it's wanted, travel light—
　　　　" Stick it."

—o—o—o—

Although it always seems your fate
To join a working party, mate,
Don't curse the sergeant, 'taint his show,
The work's to do, just grin and so—
　　　　" Stick it."

—o—o—o—

Though Belgium beer seems poor and thin,
And leaks the billet you are in ;
When you are resting, some parade
Busts all the lovely plans you've made—
　　　　" Stick it."

—o—o—o—

Though shelled by day and bombed at night,
A shirt, though lively, dry, delight
When half-way there, you think your back
Must break, you're thirsty, grub you lack—
　　　　" Stick it."

—o—o—o—

As someone said, there's no road yet
But had an end, your grinders set
On this one thing, that if you grin
And carry on, we're sure to win—
　　　　" Stick it."

JINGLES.

Although you think you've had less rest
    than any other div.
In this. or any, army —ever had
And, taking over, draw the bow,
By this and that you try to show,
You've run the war for three long years
Come cheer up sonny, dry those tears—
            You've not.

Though you have battled everywhere,
    and had most fearful loss ;
Your div. is minus one, or less than that.
You say you've lost your thousands, but
Your figures you will find " all phut : "
Your pictured dream aside is tossed,
You talk of thousands you have lost —
            You've not.

Although you think you do more work
    than any other div.
And criticise the crowd that you relieve ;
Just weigh things up and you will see,
That all are treated equally.
You think that you, and you alone
Have made secure the line we own—
            You've not.

The moral that I wish to point is not
    unkindly meant,
Though p'raps the point till now has
    been obscure ;
Don't think that others get the cake
While you the roughest always take ;
Remember when you so compare,
'Tis of YOUR team you're talking air—
            So hot.

A FEW NURSERY RHYMES.

[We must apologise for this column,
    and know our readers will forgive
    us, as it was written by our T.O.
    Its presence in the paper is due to
    the interference of war with the
    liberty of the press.—ED.]
            —o—o—o—

Little Tom Buffet,
Thought he would snuff it
When hit on the chest with a shell ;
The shell was a dud-un
So all of a sudden
He rose and is now doing well.
            —§ † §—

Ride a crocked horse
To Mobile, of course,
And see the old vet. standing there at. a
            loss ;
It may have big side-bones,
A splint or a sprain,
It's a ten to one shot if you see him
            again.
            —§ † §—
    Tommy found a little Hun,
        With whom he had a tussle ;
    He fixed his bayonet on his gun,
        And stuck it in his bussle.
            —§ † §—
Bah, bah, Quarter, have you any rum ?
Yes sir, yes sir, come ! come ! come !
A jar for the transport.
A jar for the Coy's
The rest is for the Q.M.
And all his merry boys.
            —§ † §—
    Dickory, dickory, dock,
    I've had a terrible shock ;
    For a bit of a spree,
    Fourteen days—F.P.,
    Dickory, dickory, dock.

THE REVERSE.

—o—o—o—

HAVING seen in our last number what might have been the result had some of the old poets lived in these days, let us now see how delightful it would be if these same poets could influence the everyday language of war.

—:o:—

Take for instance a Tommy with a duckboard and a knowledge of Shakespeare. We can imagine him walking up the Menin Road and discoursing thus :—

TOMMY :

To be or not to be? That is the question.
Here's nature moulded by the hand of
     man,
To be a burden borne by his own fellow,
And placed again—a weight on nature's
     breast
To bear in turn he who had once it
     borne,
Thus ease his path to slay, or maim or
     take.
And yet methinks I'm wasting time, for
     here
Comes one whose voice has power to
     move the limbs
Of loit'rers.

SERG. : Nah then! Hop it quick or else,
You'll find some F.P. waiting you me lad.

TOMMY :

Oh ! Soft-blown zephyrs flavoured well
     with rum,
Waft o'er me when I see the sergeant
     come.
               (MOVES ON.)

—:o:—

Or again ; take Zero hour and see the platoon officer throwing this off his chest :—

Awake ! For see the barrage lifts at last,
Take up your bombs. For us the die is
     cast
Come all together, top the parapet,
This moment holds the present, future,
     past.

No time to waste, to think, or wonder
     how
A hasty shot, a hurried dig and thou,
Wilt either fix the Hun or he'll fix you,
And that is for the one who's fixed enow.

—:o:—

Or again imagine a Staff Officer with a fat job and love of Browning saying, as his car splashed you from head to foot with Belgium's Best :—

Take it, only take it,
     Where you will ;
I will go on foot, or
     Better still.

—o—o—o—

Jump in here beside me
     And just say,
Where you want to go to
     And you may.

—o—o—o—

We, if you desire it
     Will proceed
For a trip to Amiens,
     And a feed.

—o—o—o—

You may have the car, dear,
     Don't mind me.
I am but a red-hat,
     Don't you see.

—:o:—

Again ! Take a sergeant with a raucous voice, and passion for Ella Wheeler Wilcox, and you might get something like this :—

Time flies. The swift hours hurry by,
You've yet to do your fatigew ;
No job of yours to reason why,
There ain't enough for me and you
Of this 'ere rum, So 'taint no good
Of cutting it in two.
And so I'll drink the lot—narpooed ;
The tin's for you.

—:o:—

If this principle was adopted throughout the Army it would make things much easier for us all, and take the rough edges off life in the trenches.

WHY NOT?

—o—o—o—

In war, as in many other things, there is so much that might be improved, and so many little inconveniences which might be done away with, if there were a better understanding on both sides. Take shelling for instance. Supposing a book of rules were drawn up by representatives of both parties, senders and receivers, something after this style,

1.—No shelling will take place between the hours of 11 p m., and 7 a.m.

2.—Parties wishing to shell will notify their opponents of the exact hour and place to be shelled by sending over a dud T.M. at a stipulated spot with a note inside.

3.—Any sheller sending his obus into any H.Q. or dug-out will forfeit two turns.

4.—A shellee on being struck by his opponent will immediately retire from the contest.

5.—A sheller pulling or slicing outside the notified area will be disqualified.

6.—The winner of the contest will be the side obtaining the greatest number of hits in the notified area.

7.—Unlimited whisky to be supplied at the 19th hole by the losing side..

Then take raids. The freedom and haphazard methods employed by the modern raider should be curtailed in common fairness to the other side, and the following code would perhaps meet a few of the requirements.

1.—A large gong will be placed in a convenient place in " No Man's Land." This will be sounded half-an-hour before Zero, at the same time signalling by the number of beats which zone the raid will be carried out in.

2.—Gas must not be used until the reasons for the failure are being discussed.

3.—Anyone throwing a bomb down a dug-out, without sounding his horn, will will lose stroke and distance, and must go back and start again.

4.—A. party rushing wilfully into its own barrage will be instantly disqualified.

5.—Barbed wire must be treated as a hazard.

One might also formulate a few rules of etiquette to be observed in raids such as :

1.—Machine guns to be considered an unsporting article of defense, and a side found using them to be sent to Coventry.

2.—It is not considered good form to regale oneself in the other side's dug-outs unless your presence there is enforced.

The foregoing ideas are only rough and could be elaborated as desired. Any suggested codes from our readers on other spheres of warfare would be welcomed by us, and put before the proper authorities for necessary action.

IN A RECENTLY-VACATED HUN DUG-OUT (APRIL 1917.)

—o—o—o—

Oft have I scorned you ; tapped you on
my boot ;
Reviled your bitterness ; complained
with ire
Your lack of name ; wished that a worthy
sire
Had fathered you, that you had been the
fruit
Of Mr Dunbill's toil, A fickle brute
Am I, for now, I miss you and desire,
Only to see the sacred, scented fire,
Glow in your bowl, dear, juicy briar
root.

—o—o—o—

These lines, I write, in pentametric
measure,
'Midst German relics, loot and food and
drink,
Arms and tobacco, bottles labelled
Munich—
I spurn the lot, the only thing, I treasure,
Has been forgotten, left behind, I think,
Safe, in the pocket of my other tunic.

C. L. P.

Correspondence.

To the Editor,
" B.E.F. Times."

Sir,

May I use your valuable space to urge on the authorities the necessity of doing something to stop the nightly disturbances. It is most annoying to the citizens of this peaceful village to have missiles, which explode with a loud detonation, thrown at them during the night hours. If nothing else can be done, surely four sausages could be hoisted holding, one at each corner, a large sheet. This would screen the moon if hoisted high enough, and thus deprive the night-hooligans of the required light to steer by. Surely, it should not be necessary for a peaceful citizen to point out methods to those highly-paid experts who are in authority.—I am, sir,

Yours faithfully,
" INDIGNANS."

ANSWERS TO CORRESPONDENTS.

JOHNNY SAVPA.—No.

Owing to pressure on our space, answers to our other correspondents are unavoidably held over.

THE "BETTER TIMES."

WITH WHICH ARE INCORPORATED

The Wipers Times, The "New Church" Times,

The Kemmel Times, The Somme-Times,

& The B.E.F. Times.

No. 1. Vol. 1. November, 1918. Price 1 Franc.

EUROPEAN THEATRE OF VARIETIES.

THIS WEEK AND TILL FURTHER NOTICE.

Professor FOCH & his Performing DOVE.

Signor Pleni Potentiario
WILL SING
"THE ONLY WAY"
AND
"THE END OF A PERFECT DAY."

WILLEM VAN HOHENZOLLERN
IN
"MY OLD DUTCH."

Book Early Prices as Usual.
Safe From Air Raids.

EDITORIAL.

"ICI NOUS sommes encore!" As French that is probably rotten, but we have just found a complete outfit and are naturally jubilant that we can carry out our threat of carrying on a paper till the Hun is down and out. The old staff has rallied round us (with many regrettable vacancies), and Mr. Teech Bomas will retain his appointment at his previous enormous salary. Some new members have been enrolled, and we hope to receive the support accorded to the predecessors of the *Better Times*. With the present publication we are going to make an effort to reproduce illustrations As they will be hand engraved on woodblock, will intending artists please stick to line efforts. Our new paper is born in very different circumstances to the old *Wipers Times*, and it is strange that we should get our new outfit during an advance over the same country in which the old one was lost last March. We are the gainers by the exchange, as the new one is a much finer machine. Yet the old one held many memories for us, and we did not enthuse over losing it. Within four days of capturing the town where we found the new press we brought out an evening paper called the *Avesnes Advertiser*, although the Hun had done his best to prevent any effort at journalism by shifting all the type to his melting-station and filling the office with gas. However all the type is now in process of sorting, and we have a fine selection. The war itself needs no comment, and a few more efforts should bust the Hun completely. Anyway it seems pretty certain that everyone is out to finish the job properly, which is all very satisfactory. We hope that budding journalists will not wait to be asked to send along copy. Our letter box is open day and night, and the same fabulous rates will be paid for stuff used namely—copies of the paper.

The Editor.

SOME HAVE FAME THRUST UPON THEM.

—o—o—o—

'Twas a sentry young on a lonely post
    And he scanned the earth and sky,
When he was aware of a red tabbed throng
    Which came a-trotting by.

—o—o—o—

Now the leading wight was a general old,
    And the rest, some far, some nigh,
Came panting on in the deuce of a sweat;
    The sentry wondered why.

—o—o—o—

But the general stopped and he spake these words,
    "So you watch the earth and sky!
Do you know that the fate of an empire hangs
    On just *your* watchful eye"

—o—o—o—

'Twas a grubby fist that the general grasped
    "You'll be proud lad by and bye,
That you shook my hand on a summers day;
    Your Corps Commander *I*.

—o—o—o—

When the sentry left to his lonely post,
    He winked at the earth and sky,
Far off in the trenches a mile away,
    Faint streaks of red flashed by.

EDITORIAL.

(Continued.)

OWING to the lapse of time between the beginning and end of setting up this number (a lapse which was unavoidable owing to the way Fritz hit the trail for the homeland) it has become necessary to add a few words, hence—*this*. Since writing and printing the Editorial page Fritz has turned it up, and our swords are going to be made into ploughshares or something of the sort. It seems a pity as the back end of the war was the best part we have struck so far, and we only had two months of it compared with three years of the muddy end of the stick. However everyone is heartily glad the ghastly affair is well over, and the future alone will show if there will ever be another number of this paper. The Editor and Sub-Editor send their congratulations to all members of the Division, particularly to the few who are original members and have followed the Division through all its vicissitudes. For those who are not with us, but lie in France and Belgium, our reverence and love be with them and they will never be forgotten. From September 14 to November '18 is a long span, and the old Division has seen many changes, luckily few for the worse. We are going to make an effort to keep the paper going till Peace is signed, sealed and delivered, and so we continue to pester all and sundry for copy.

The Editor.

EXTRACT FROM THE BOOK OF TOMAR-SAT-KINS.

—:o:—

And it came to pass at eleven hours of the eleventh day of the eleventh month there was silence throughout the Land of the Westernfront. And no one did loose a gun, no, not so much as a pip-squeak did go off. And the heart of Tomar-Sat-Kins was glad in him so that he did give praise saying " Wotto, no tarf, and the Land of Blighty shall know me *some* more." For he did know that the time of the Hunnites was come, and that peace would shortly come throughout the land.

THE FOREBODINGS OF A C.O.

—:o:—

"AND so most of us are, or shortly will be, out of work! Thrown on the mercies of a cruel hard world without the tender care of our foster-mothers, the corporals, sergeants, or whoever may have been *in loco parentis* during these years. Shall we all be able to resist the snares and temptations or will the guard room become, in memory, a desirable haven of rest, compared with the trouble which most of us will rush into."

It is thoughts such as these which are furrowing the brows and greying the hair of most Commanding Officers. A Commanding Officer suddenly visualises his family thrown out of his fatherly care and into the snares and pitfalls which are waiting. Can you wonder at the pale and haggard look on his face? See the troubled eye, the furrowed brow, the greying temple. He gazes in the fire and pictures his Second-in-Command in the clutches of a Syren, his guileless Company Commanders stripped and broken by the first gang of crooks to meet them, his Adjutant in gaol for forgery, his Quartermaster in a home for incurable inebriates, his M.O. a drug fiend, his N.C.O.'s and men victims of harpies, crooks and other human vampires; all these, his children of the last four years he sees twisted, broken and writhing. His Subalterns, boys four years ago, plunged straight from school to war, and now to be plunged from war to the world. Can you wonder that he shudders for them and his eye grows dim, and his mouth takes on a yearning droop. Pity him then,

"As a drooping lily "

and mock not that age has gripped him 'Tis not the years that make his figure as a drooping lily, that make his face so pale and lined.

CEASE FIRE.

And so at last it's *fini* !
Can you understand the silence ? Are you
waiting for the barrage ?
When the fateful hour of zero comes and
you're " across the bags,"
Are your ears and senses straining for the
vicious sound of shelling
When it's " down into a shell hole and God
help the one who lags."

—:o:—

And now the Hun's " napooed " !
Can you forget those early days of
undiluted hell ?
That scared your soul and made you doubt
your God.
When " Wipers " though a deadly rat-
infested, muddy shell,
Seemed a Heaven when the mud of Hooge
you trod.

—:o:—

And now " apres la guerre ! "
For years you've heard that sentence tossed
from taunting maid to man,
Heard it chanted right from Nieuport to
Lorraine,
In a hovel up in Belgium when your soul
was sick with war,
Or at Mazingarbe, Aubigny, or Avesnes.

—:o:—

" Oofs ! ! Compree, eggs ? "
Will you e'er forget the jargon ? Will these
four years pass away
Till their memory is but an ugly dream ?
Yet I would not lose the friends one found
when life was less worth while
Than I had thought that life could ever
seem.

—:o:—

" Hell ! She's ditched ! "
In the future years when dreaming of those
nights along the roads.
When the rattle on the pavé drove you mad,
When you couldn't hear " it " coming, and
the first thing that you knew
Was that Jim and George, your pals, had
" got it bad."

" Curse this corner ! "
Oh ! that bloody reeking pavé round by
Wipers and Potije
Where the corpses lined the sides, half hid
in mud
Men and horses, and the litter of the stores
they brought is spread
Through the night, while greedy Belgium
laps up blood.

—:o:—

" Zero is at four ! "
Loos, the Somme, Messines and Vimy,
Passchendaele and Bourlon Wood,
The stink and bloody swelter of them all ;
The acrid fumes of shelling, gas, and death,
God send that we
May forget at least what we would not
recall.

—:o:—

" Hostilities cease at 11 a.m. ! "
Though these words marked hours which
hist'ry well may hold divide the world
And the centuries in half by all they mean,
Yet our brains could not conceive it, and
the Column plodded on—
You cannot blot out years as from a
screen !

—:o:—

" Rations oop ! "
When you're beat and wet and hungry, cold
and don't care if you're dead.
Do you think that future hopes can ease the
ache ?
When you'd sell your soul for warmth,
just want to sleep and sleep, and so
You just don't care a damn if you don't
wake.

—:o:—

'Tis the small things make one's world up,
and the greatest slither by,
'Tis " the canteen's closed " " late rations "
make you curse ;
What do emperors and empires going bust
concern you when
The mud and rain and filth are getting
worse ?

—:o:—

" *Dis-miss !* '
Yet I think this lack of boasting and this
calm, serene and still,
Mark a deeper sense of thankfulness and
pride,
Pride—not in our own achievements, but
in Britain and her fate
In our women, proved and tested, true and
tried

THE SOLDIER'S FRIEND.

—o—o—o—

(In this column we will endeavour to cope with the problems that are troubling the soldiers.)

—o—o—o—

Private Stickit of Northampton writes :—

"Dear Sir.—I have been told that if a man has no work after the War, that the Government is going to pay him some money each week for a whole year. As I mean to have a long holiday after I am demobilised could I have a lump sum so as I could get married?"

—:o:—

Yes! Private Sticket, you will be able to have as much as you want. There will be a quarter-master's stores opened in every big town, and you will be able to obtain money on indent through the usual channels.

—:o:—

One Pip writes :—

"Dear Sir :—I was at the Front in 1914. Through all those awful months I stuck to my post and came through without a scratch. There were six of us at the Base, and we all managed to get through. We are writing to you to see if nothing can be done to stop these later fighters from wearing our Star"

"1914."

—:o:—

Well, "1914," we will exert our influence to stop an injustice being done.

—:o:—

Lce-Cpl. Jones (Buffs) writes :—

"Dear Sir.—I hear that the people who joined early are going to be demobilised first. I think this is very unjust. Surely those who joined first were much more eager to join the Army than we who were combed out later. As they were more eager to join, it must have been because they liked it. Therefore they should be demobilised much later than we who joined up reluctantly."

—:o:—

Yes! Jones. There's a lot in what you say, and we will put your view before the proper authorities.

—:o:—

Many answers are unavoidably held over owing to lack of space, but we will endeavour to answer them in our next issue

---

CAN YOU SOLVE THIS??

100,000 FRANCS IN PRIZES.

FIRST PRIZE : 50,000 Francs in Cash
2nd do. : 25,000 Francs in Cash
3rd do. : 12,750 Francs in Cash

Several Prizes of 1,000 Francs and 500 Francs.

ALL YOU HAVE TO DO!

Fill in the missing letters, and send your solution and 50 francs to the Editor :

MAKE H·· WHILE THE S·N S·IN·S.

All solutions to be sent in by 12·00 hours on the 31st December.

AUX REPATRIÉES.

We are coming! We are coming!!
And the hour of peace is near,
Here we greet you with our homage,
And we bid you cease from fear.

—o—o—o—

You have drained your cup of anguish,
You have plumbed the depths of grief,
You have prayed each hopeless morning,
For the long-deferred relief.

—o—o—o—

We have marked with kindling spirit
All the traces of the beast,
And the Hun shall bear the branding
From "The Highest" to the least.

—o—o—o—

Brute in mind, and heart and body
He shall know the outcast's shame;
But the crowning of his Kultur
Is your curse upon his name.

—o—o—o—

Ruined homes and hearts nigh broken
Where the Boche has found his prey,
Left with only eyes to weep with,
Dear ones dead or far away.

—o—o—o—

For your sorrows take our pity,
For your dead accept our praise;
For the past of dire oppression,
Lo, we bring you brighter days.

—o—o—o—

Courage! you shall have your freedom
And your tears are not in vain.
For we bring you your deliv'rance
From your terror and your bane.

—o—o—o—

Count your woes a passing nightmare
Hideous, yet an evil trance.
From the welter of your trials
There shall rise a fairer France.

—o—o—o—

France, all fairer for your sorrows,
France, all nobler for your grief,
We are coming! We are coming!
And we bring you your relief.
THE PADRE.

RACING.

A SUCCESSFUL meeting was held on Wednesday, October 30th, under the aegis of the M.G. Battalion, and an interesting programme of five events was got through with commendable despatch. First-class weather conditions prevailed, and the course was thronged with the flower of the local chivalry The third race, which was the only open event, attracted a fair field, and about half-a-dozen animals eventually came under the starter's orders, all trained to the hour. The services of all the most famous jockeys had been secured, so the chances looked very open. As the time for the race drew near the excitement was intense, and I heard many large wagers freely offered and taken over the railings, every horse being well supported, though with slight preference possibly for Capt. Pincher's chestnut The gate eventually went up to a magnificent start, and there seemed little to choose between the bunch till the distance was reached, when the favourite with the Captain up drew clear, and won by about four lengths from Shid, who was using his whip. We hear on the best authority that the result was a big surprise to a certain clever division who had a real good thing to slip for this race. It is further rumoured that—anyway for the time being they've taken the knock.

The Band of the Coldstream Guards played delightful music on the lawn during the afternoon, and added to what everyone felt to be a delightful day.

"Nott
Mit
Uns!"

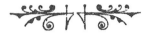

There was a young man of Avesnes,
Took a stroll down a long shady lesnes,
   He trod on a dud
   Half hidden in mud . . . * !
He never will do it agesnes.

How the hours crept round the clock
Till we got our Yankee Doc.
Now the time slips gaily by,
List and I will tell you why!
When the war begins to bore us
Then our Yank joins in the chorus,
And (though p'raps not quite *de rigeur*)
Yet the ripples of his figure
As he yields to merriment
Makes us think the time well spent,
Sad must be the day and black
When we see our old Doc's back.

TOTTERING TO A FALL.

—:o:—

By TEECH BOMAS.

—:o:—

And so we broke through the line and the pride of Germany's colossal army was humbled to the dust. As I write the situation is liquid and I must tear round the battlefield several times more before I give a clear account of what has happened. I must tell you of how the North Southshires crossed the Canal. Every man was equipped with a pair of large springs under his feet. and a pair of wings strapped to his shoulders. At zero plus 5 the whole sprang on the bank and were carried over by these appliances, thus completely surprising the Huns. On they went in leaps and bounds, and in two hours the stream of prisoners began to pour in. I saw thousands myself and had I not been so busy I should have been able to see thousands more. Anyway. the vaunted Blindenburg line is shattered and we are through. I walked through Valenciennes this morning, and the Hun shells were still falling on every part of the town. I hurried through to the foremost battle-fronts although all inside me cried out to linger and study the condition of the town. I felt that I must be able to get you the latest situation so, having wired Foch that all was going well, on I went. Now I met Huns singly and in twos or threes putting up their hands. The most touching episodes occurred with the civilians who had been relieved by our advance. I was kissed on both cheeks by all and sundry, and although I was much embarrassed yet how could one stop these poor people. The situation is, as I repeat fluid, and until it sets it is impossible to tell you more. I am off to the battle again —I love it.

Teech Bomas.

LETTERS TO THE EDITOR.

—o—o—o—

To the Editor
The Better Times.

Sir,
Why shouldn't we who told our friends to enlist wear some modification of the 1914 Star? Surely our timely words were the cause of raising the first hundred thousand and ought to have some recognition.

Yours etc.,
CUTHBERT CUSHIJOBBE.
Dept. F
Ministry of Fancywork,
Hotel Velvet, W.C. 14

—o—o—o—

To the Editor.

Sir,
Your correspondence re the 1914 15 Star interests me very much I have never laughed so much since the day when father lost his false teeth overboard on the good ship *Angostura* in 1912.

Yours etc.,
A. E. G. BEAMS.

—o—o—o—

To the Editor.

Sir,
I didn't come out to France till 1918, and then managed to click for a job at the Base. Don't you think I ought to have the 1918 Star and Garter to show how clever I've been?

Yours etc.,
J. M. WANGLEUR,
A.P,O. 15.

—o—o—o—

To the Editor.

Sir,
I tried to enlist early in 1915 and was rejected on account of my teeth. I got a new set fitted at my own expense and managed to pass the doctor in June 1916 Surely there should be some sort of Star—say a 1915 16—for me! Or again, the "Spirit was willing but the Flesh (teeth) weak"; couldn't we wear a badge with that quotation engraved upon it?

Yours etc.,
O. MYE-MOLARS,
94th General Hospital,
France.

THE XMAS PRESENT.

—o—o—o—

German Plenipotentiary receives a "Special Peace-Signing" Fountain Pen.

—o—o—o—

TRICOLOR.

—:o:—

Mid shriek and hiss of falling shell,
The torn Earth trembling, torture-riven,
God's face obscured, the World a Hell,
Man, like a puppet, onward driven,
On through the battle's smoke and roar,
Rushing with bayonet fixed, he saw
RED.

In quiet home of rest and peace.
Far from the conflict's blare and rattle,
Where wounds are healed and strivings cease,
For weary warriors worn by battle,
Mid sweet and smiling V.A.D.'s,
Waking from dreams of death, he sees
WHITE.

The time goes on, he leaves his cot
And hobbles round with aid of crutches,
The old familiar sights he'll spot,
The old familiar things he touches:
He little recks the scar he bears,
As taking his walks abroad, he wears
BLUE.

THE
"BETTER TIMES."

WITH WHICH ARE INCORPORATED

The Wipers Times, The "New Church" Times,

The Kemmel Times, The Somme-Times,

& The B.E.F. Times.

No. 2. Vol. 1.   December, 1918.   Price 1 Franc.

EDITORIAL.

" When this blooming war is over,
Oh ! how happy we shall be ;
When we get our civvy clothes on
No more soldiering for we."
(Expurgated Soldier's Song.)

RE we? and shall we ? The end of the War none of us will ever regret, but there will be a lot connected with the last four years that we shall miss.   A lot of us can remember blue-clad mobs wandering (one cannot call it marching) down English lanes and streets singing the above.   This was in the days before khaki was obtainable. And many of us can trace those same mobs through the various stages of camp, Aldershot, B.E.F., until to-day when we know them as soldiers, many of them veterans, beribboned, but still singing the same old grouse. We cannot say that the majority of us took to soldiering kindly, but now that it is all over and we shall soon " have our civvy clothes on," the reversion will be tinged with many regrets. One cannot but remark on the absolute apathy with which the end was received over here.   England seems to have had a jollification, but here one saw nothing but a disinterested interest in passing events.   Perhaps that was because the end came without the expected culmination crash, and the decisive battle was spread over many months, and so became an indefinite action and not a "show." Anyway though some may be sorry it's over, there is little doubt that the line men are *not*, as most of us have been cured of any little illusions we may have had about the pomp and glory of war, and know it for the vilest disaster that can befall mankind.   We must apologise for the delay in issuing *No. 1 Better Times*.   This was due to the nomadic existence we have been leading since the acquisition of the press which takes a day to set up and a day to take down, so that at least four days in one place are necessary before it's worth while unpacking. However, now we are established we hope to make our paper a weekly issue, and to print 1,000 copies. To do this more support must be forthcoming, and copy must roll in. So will Battn. Commanders and O's./C. units please do their best to make productive the shy and retiring subaltern. Cox will not be able to stand the strain of three month's peace warfare unless the time of subalterns is occupied by the less-expensive vices, poetry etc. If it could be done we should like to run a daily paper in conjunction, as we have the loan of another press. So will all the ex-journalists in the Div. please volunteer their services. This is our Xmas Number, and we take this opportunity of wishing all members of the Division a Merry Xmas, etc.

The Editor.

THE FIFTH AND LAST.

In '14 when the war was young
By military ardour stung
We'd donned the khaki, and begun
To train for smashing up the Hun ;
Our tutors, though assuming lore
And dishing out wild tales of gore,
Knew just as much of war as we—
Which was *narpoo*, you must *compree*.

At 6 a.m. each winter's morn
The Front at Brighton looked forlorn
Yet not one tenth forlorn as we,
Who willy-nilly did P.T.
With mingled curses, sobs and groans
We dislocated all our bones,
Yet suffered gladly all that tosh
Thinking 'twould help to smash the
    "boche."

—o—o—o—

Our next Noël was passed in France,
At war by then we looked askance,
We'd sampled some of it at Loos
And for its charms had little use ;
We'd tried St Eloi and The Bluff
And thought the Huns uncouth and rough,
Yet things all panned out for the best
That Xmas Day found us "at rest."

—o—o—o—

The Natal Day of '16 found
Us back at Loos, the same old round
Of trenches, minnies, shells and mud,
Lord ! how we'd got to hate the thud
Of shrieking hunks of metal, which
Just passed your ear and struck your ditch,
And to us all just then it seemed
This was not war of which we'd dreamed.

—o—o—o—

Another twelve months rolled away
Each month a year, each hour a day,
A plethora of blood and woe
The net result "in statu quo ";
That Christmas Day itself we'd got
The soldier's dream—a cushy spot.
St Quentin just in front you'd find,
The old Somme battlefield behind.

—o—o—o—

By then we'd given up surmise
When peace would come and in what guise,
Nor wondered if it were the last
Noël which would at war be passed,
Just spared some breath to curse the Hun
For all he did, for all he'd done,
For all he yet might do, *àpres*
We'd celebrate our Christmas Day.

—o—o—o—

And now we've reached the last Noël
The job completely done and well,
We've done with mud and shells, and
    stench,
Hope ne'er again to see a trench,
No more to hear the crumps come in,
The whizzbang's shriek, the minnie's din.
The long last years have been well worth
If once again we've " Peace on Earth."

Scrap the pip-squeak, sixty pounders,
Six and eight inch, gun or how.,
Soon we'll be back playing rounders
Gone are all their uses now.
Pack away the good old sausage
Turn Tock Emmas into pans,
Now we're changed from war to school
days
Even Wilhelm's changed to Hans.

IN THE PINK.
—:o:—

Dear Father, and Mother,
    I hope and I pray,
(I'm writing in pencil, I've run out of ink)
That this letter finds you as it leaves me to-day
    In the pink.
They told us to capture the Violet line,
    Which we did after Zero, before you could
        wink,
Then we scuppered some Boches preparing
        to dine
    In the pink.

Oh! Mabel's divine in the emerald green,
And Maudie in brown with the trimming
        of mink.
But Kitty for me is the absolute Queen
    In the pink.

Some sigh for the scent of the lily or rose,
Mignonette or narcissus or orchid; I think
That the sweetest of perfumes will always
        repose
    In the pink.

Some chivvy the fox in the ratcatcher kit,
Whilst others in black from publicity shrink,
But you'll come if you really intend to be IT
    In the pink.
    —0—0—0—

MEMORIES.
—:o:—

Do you remember, dearest, that day upon
    Hampstead Heath,
With the blue, blue sky above us, and the
    green, green grass beneath ;
We talked of our love together,
Ah! sweet was the old refrain :
And then we talked of the weather,
And hoped that it wouldn't rain.

We strolled through the shady woodland.
    and down by the babbling stream.
While the birds in the trees above us kept
    murmuring love's young dream ;
Our two hearts were one indeed, dear,
As we walked through the leafy glade,
And then we went off for a feed dear,
Of biscuits and lemonade.

When the beautiful time was ended,
    together we walked away,
As the shadows of night descended at the
    close of a summer's day ;
We thought of the Summer Sun, love,
How brightly it shone for us,
And then we commenced to run, love,
To catch the last homeward bus.

                R. W. M.

BON CHANCE.

—o—o—o—

As this is our last number the Editor and Sub Editor would like to take this opportunity of thanking all those who have so kindly helped us with the paper. We had intended to carry on till we had all received the order of the bowler hat, but as most of the printing staff are miners and consequently going almost at once, it will be impossible to do any further numbers. To all of you the best wishes for Xmas and the future, and hearty thanks for your aid and support.

(*Signed*) F. J. ROBERTS, Editor
J. H. PEARSON, Sub-Editor.

AT LAST.

—o—o—o—

"Our Cavalry have crossed the Rhine."—*Daily Paper.*

—:o:—

Our Cavalry have crossed the
Rhine,
Ring out the bells with peal on
peal,
Our Cavalry have crossed the
Rhine,
Those words to all of us appeal;
No blatant music-hall refrain
Or ill-timed boast of what we'd
do
To smash the Kaiser and his
train,
And then to "Wind a Watch
Up" too.
Yet words which bridge four
years of gloom
Which made us doubt the sun
could shine,
Throughout the World the
message boom :—
Our Cavalry have crossed the
Rhine.

THE HORRORS OF PEACE.

—:o:—

We have had a good look at the horrors of war, and now we are undergoing another sort of frightfulness. What a life! Can anyone tell us of a nice war where we could get work and so save our remaining hair from an early greyness? 11.00 hours on the eleventh of November was zero hour, and the redhats attacked in mass. The barrage of paper fell right on our trenches, and mixed with the H.E was gas in enormous quantities. The supports were rushed into the orderly room in time to save the line from giving, Numbers are against us Also the disposition of the enemy is much in his favour. His left flank rests on Education, and his right on recreation. He has carefully selected shock-masses of " Returns," and with these is rapidly undermining our morale. We are taking up a defensive position in various towns, and there we are going to hold on at all costs. Meanwhile we are drawing up a list of our "fourteen points," and these may form the basis of a suitable armistice. As I remarked before, if anyone knows of a *nice* war, or if one can be arranged, we hope we shall be allowed first call.

Should you happen choice to have
Would you be a Jugo-Slav?
Or, a disappointed cove, acknowledge you're a Czecho-Slovak!
Would you if you'd not a groat
Care to own yourself a Croat?
Fain would I be any one
Than to own myself a Hun!

LETTERS TO THE EDITOR.

—o—o—o—

THE 1914 STAR.

To the Editor,
The Better Times.

Sir —I feel I cannot let this 1914 Star discussion pass without airing my little grievance. My husband has got the 1914 Star, and the red, white and blue ribbon clashes most horribly with my cerise blouse.

What can I do? I am most perplexed about it.

Am I to dye the blouse, dye the ribbon, or get a new husband?

Yours etc.,
A CONTEMPTIBLE'S WIFE.
9a Suburban Villas, Peckham.

—o—o—o—

To the Editor.

Sir.—My husband is a Corps Commander who has a very large number of decorations; in fact there is no more room left for any more ribbons.

It is rumoured that he is to be presented very soon with the O.B.E. and another Home and Colonial Order.

I propose therefore to make a flap, with ribbons on both sides. The flaps will bounce up and down as he walks, thus shewing either side alternately.

I thought this idea worth mentioning for the benefit of other worried wives of much decorated Corps Commanders.

Yours etc.,
INGENUITY.
27 Murkie Mansions, W.46.

—o—o—o—

To the Editor.

Sir.—Surely the practice of putting thru-pennybits, silver charms, etc. in Christmas puddings ought to be stopped. Last Xmas I was dining with some friends and we, of course, had a Xmas pudding; but what do you think I got in my portion of pudding? A thrupennypiece, a 50 centime note (very dirty one), a Bosche cartridge, a piece of film 2·25 inches long, a cigar stump and 3 carpet tacks.

It is a dangerous practice as well as very insanitary. This view is endorsed by my doctor, who performed the operation after-wards.

Yours etc.,
WILLIAM WOOLFIT.
St Agnes' Convalescent Home
Seasyde super-Mare.

To the Editor.

Sir.—I think it is seasonable to bring to the notice of both young and old a new Christmas game I have invented. Anyone can play it; it is so simple. At present I call it "Stick-it-Girls," but perhaps some of your readers may be able to suggest a better name.

This is all it is : the ladies all go out of the room leaving the gentlemen to tie all their walking sticks and umbrellas together with a piece of short twine. One of the gentlemen goes to the door and says "Catchemquick!" whereupon the ladies rush in and untie the sticks. It is such fun, and merry peals of laughter always greet the lady who fails to say "Gallawalla" if she knocks a chair down in the rush.

Yours etc.,
B.F.
Lady Airbrane's Asylum for
Feeble Gentlefolk,
Chelmsford.

THE DEMOBILISATION

SMILE!

EYEWASH.

"Good morning! I salute you as I rush up
    on my charger
Which is thoroughly and daily disinfected,
The impression I shall make will be pro-
    portionately larger
When a greater body-guard I have collected.
Now is your fly-trap grease-proof; are all
    my orders framed,
Have you put chloride of lime upon the ham,
Have your you-know-what's been thin-
    gummy and daily whatsernamed
But, by the way do you know who I am?
Chorus.—I'm General Sir Chloride H.K.L.M.
    Bunter, Bart.,
You'll have to say it slowly for a start,
    You can write and tell your mother
    Your father, sister, brother,
Your sons and daughters, uncles, aunts,
    and they can tell each other
That of all the Corps Commanders
    Who command in France or Flanders,
You've never met one who is half as smart
    Or so absolutely grand
    As he who shakes your hand—
General Sir Chloride H.K.L.M Bunter,
    Bart.

—:o:—

Ah! now here a fly I notice, which is flat
    against my orders,
'Tis the cause of all the P.U.O. and similar
    disorders,
    If it once gets on the meat
    The result will be trench feet,
You must try and recollect the few sugges-
    tions I have made,
    If you've read your C.R.O.
    You certainly must know
That on no account will any fly be forward
    of Brigade,
    Now get a piece of suet
    Stick a pin or needle through it
And camouflage the front to look like jam,
    He'll settle—exit fly
    He'll see the point and die,
Are you sure you still remember who I am?
Chorus—I'm General Sir Chloride H.K.L.M.
    Bunter, Bart., *etc.*

Now let me see your transport, are your
    mules in good condition?
You must cheer them up if they're inclined
    to fret,
A blotting pad per head would be an
    excellent addition
To dry them if they ever start to sweat;
And now, when shoeing animals I'll tell you
    what to do,
You must always be as gentle as a lamb,
Just make the shoes of biscuit tins and stick
    them on with glue,
    Farrier, do you know who I am?
Chorus.—I'm General Sir Chloride H.K.L.M.
    Bunter, Bart., *etc.*

—:o:—

And now we'll see the baths. Are you sure
    they're quite hygenic?
Does the band play when the men do their
    ablutions,
Are the pictures on the wall allegorical or
    scenic,
Are they well washed with bi-carbonate
    solutions,
Are you absolutely sure the men undress
    before immersion,
Do they dry themselves with bathmat, towel
    or soap,
If you'll dip their clothes in green-cross gas
    you'll notice the desertion
Of all the lice. The men know me, I hope,
Chorus.—I'm General Sir Chloride H.K.L.M.
    Bunter, Bart, *etc.*

               ALBERTA.

War is full of quaint surprises,
Huns are never free from guile,
All the world—full of surmises
Watches William with a smile.

Printed &
Published by
Sherwood, Forester &
Co., Ltd.
B.E.F.